I. THE ACCURACY OF "ISLAMIC FUNDAMENTALISM" IN TURKEY

Author Nazih Ayubi has suggested many Western scholars have erroneously concluded that most Muslims have rejected the notion of the modern state in favor of some Islamic political entity.[1] In turn, often through academically untenable positions expounding the inflexibility and antagonistic nature of Islam to the state, these same scholars have influenced Western society's perceptions of the Islamic World. According to Ayubi, some of these positions have included such fallacies as the belief that the concept of the nation-state has no tradition in the Islamic World. Another is that a heavy "intellectual legacy", such as the classical Muslim view of dividing the world between the dar al-islam (realm of peace) and dar al-harb (realm of war), inhibits more modern political concepts.[2] The results of scholarly misperceptions and warnings about Islam and politics in the Islamic World are now popularly referred to as "Islamic fundamentalism", or a similar term.

---

[1]Nazih Ayubi, _Political Islam: Religion and Politics in the Arab World_ (London; Routledge, 1991), 42.

[2]Ibid., 44-46.

1

Western notions of "fundamentalism" in Islam are heavily influenced by 20th century movements in American Protestantism, which espouses a literalist interpretation of the Bible.[3] This term, when applied to Islam implies that a difference exists between Muslims who do not hold a literalist view of the Quran, and those who do. In fact, there is no such dichotomy in Islamic culture as the Quran is considered by all Muslims to be the literal word of God.[4] Furthermore, as Professor John Esposito points out, this term is associated with pejorative concepts like extremism, fanaticism and anti-Americanism, among others.[5] The inaccurate application of this term is symbolic then of Western misperceptions about this important phenomenon.

As mistakes are being made in Western circles at such a basic level in regard to understanding "Islamic activism,"[6] one must question the accuracy of the accepted wisdom expounded on other issues related to this topic. For

---

[3]For an excellent discussion on the use of this term read John L. Esposito, The Islamic Threat: Myth or Reality?, (Oxford: Oxford University Press, 1992), 7-8.

[4]Ibid., 7-8, and Professor Glenn Robinson, NS 4300, Naval Postgraduate School, 24 Feb 93.

[5]Ibid., 7-8.

[6]This alternative term is suggested by Professor Robinson. I will use this term and others, to include the now popularized "fundamentalism," to connote the notion of a politically active and sometimes violent Islamic movement.

instance, is there truly a radical Islamic revival spreading throughout the entire Middle East, Central Asia, and elsewhere, as implied in the popular media? In an April 1992 article in The Economist, the message was clear that an "anti-Western" Islamic revival was occurring in numerous countries.[7] This article displayed a map of North Africa, the Middle East and Central Asia, with references to 17 countries having some level of disturbing Islamic activity. Even the Republic of Turkey, which has been officially secular since Ataturk amended the constitution in 1928 to remove the reference to Turkey as an Islamic state,[8] and with arguably the most entrenched Western values of any Muslim country, is implied to be threatened. This is not a novel claim. The Washington Post also ran a story in April 1992, using this same map of the world with its 17 highlighted Muslim countries under the shadow of Islamic fundamentalism. The caption for Turkey read as follows:

> The Welfare Party, seeking closer ties with the
> Islamic world, ran in the October 1991 election in
> alliance with two nationalist parties, the alliance

---

[7]"Islam Resumes its March," The Economist (4-10 Apr 92); 47-48.

[8]Sydney Nettleton Fischer and William Ochsenwald, The Middle East, A History, 4th ed., (New York: McGraw-Hill Publishing Company, 1990), 406.

won 17 percent of the vote but no seats [sic]. Several
small fundamentalist groups engage in terrorism.[9]

Claims about the threat of a resurgent Islam to Turkey
have not come from the press alone. In 1984, one Western
think-tank noted that secularism in Turkey, "has been
eroding."[10] More recently, another Western pundit described
Turkey as "quasi-secular."[11] Is this to imply it is more
Islamic than secular, or that it is slipping towards some
concept of an Islamic state? David Barchard, writing for
The World Today, wrote this pessimistic note in 1990 about
Islam in Turkey:

> However, other intellectuals are now beginning to argue
> that the intelligentsia must try and create a
> dialogue with Turkey's resurgent Islamic movements,
> even if-as seems fairly clear-one of the goals of those
> movements is to eliminate secular and westernizing
> values from Turkish political life.[12]

Are these and other assertions about the extent of
Islamic activism in Turkey accurate? Should there be

---

[9]This caption is incorrect, as the Welfare Party alliance won
62 seats. This was later corrected. The source for this map was
listed as The Economist. Dave Coor, "Islam: Politics and Piety,"
The Washington Post, 26 Apr 1992, A28.

[10]Daniel Pipes, "Fundamentalist Muslims and U.S. Policy," The
Heritage Foundation International Briefing, (Washington, D.C.: The
Heritage Foundation), 10 Aug 1984.

[11]Martha Brill Olcott, "Central Asia's Catapult to
Independence," Foreign Affairs, Vol. 71, No. 2 (Summer 1992): 125.

[12]David Barchard, "Turkey's Troubled Prospect," The World
Today, Vol. 46, No. 6, (Jun 1990): 109.

concern that Turkey, a strong U.S. ally and model of modernity in the Middle East and greater Muslim World, could, at one extreme, eventually resemble its theocratic neighbor Iran? Or, as Ayubi and others might argue, is this simply another unfounded fear based on fallacies, ignorance, and an uncritical acceptance of information expounding a negative image of Islam? To anyone who follows events in Turkey, there have been obvious signs of Islamic resurgence in the last few years. But, do these Islamic sentiments necessarily reflect "Islamic fundamentalism," as this term is understood in the West?

Clearly, there are expressions of Islamic activism in Turkey. It would be surprising if there were not some degree of Islamic expression in a country with a population of 58 million people, 99 percent of whom are Muslim.[13] However, the evidence being used to demonstrate the extent of Islamic activism in Turkey today, like many aspects of the Middle East and Islam, is being taken out of context. It is my thesis that the evidence for warnings of a serious Islamic challenge to Ataturk's secular legacy are weak. I will argue this point in the first section of this paper by examining and placing in perspective recent political and

---

[13]PC Globe, Version 4.0 (New York, N.Y.: Copyright 1990, PC Globe, Inc.) Citing World Population Data Sheet, Washington: Population Bureau, 1990.

social factors construed to be signs of Islamic activism in Turkey. Before proceeding with an examination of the political and social evidence, it is first necessary to define the distinct elements which fall under the rubric of Islamic fundamentalism.

A. NECESSARY DISTINCTIONS AMONG ISLAMIC GROUPS

In the legitimate concern over the rise of Islamic movements which conduct or threaten hostile acts against the interests of the U.S. and its Western and Middle Eastern allies, the return by many Muslims to the fold of Islam has been erroneously equated to an increase in Islamic fundamentalism. The two are not synonymous. The problem stems from a combination of mistakes. One is the excessive and wrongful application of the term fundamentalism to numerous entities undeserving of this negative title. Another is the failure to make appropriate distinctions between the sundry of Islamic groups. Such distinctions should involve the separation between truly threatening movements based on distorted, fringe interpretations of Islam, and those Muslims adhering or returning to the traditional values embodied in their religion for personal reasons.

To a certain degree this distinction can be made by recognizing that there are social and political components grouped under the umbrella of fundamentalism. In general, social movements involving Islam may simply reflect an individual's desire to return to his religion. Such is presently the case in Central Asia, where Islam was repressed both under the Russians and Soviets. As Oliver Roy of the French National Center for Scientific Research in Paris said:

> Since 1988, Islam has become visible. Mosques have re-opened, mullahs are active, and religious schools are under construction. This does not mean that a wave of fundamentalism has engulfed Central Asia; Islam had always remained active in the underground and has now made a comeback.[14]

Similar social groups desiring a return to Islam can not be discounted in Turkey. As in Central Asia, the return of Islam to Turkey may reflect an attempt by some Turks to recapture their religious heritage which, if not in opposition to Ataturk's principles, was certainly eclipsed by them in public.

In regard to Islamic political movements, further recognition must be made between those seeking to reform the state, while maintaining its essential entity, from those who challenge the state system. Some actors may be

---

[14]Oliver Roy, "Central Asian Republics: New Elements in Regional Politics," in Balance of Power in Central and Southwest Asia, ed. Steven R. Dorr and Lt. Neysa M. Slater, USN (Defense Intelligence Agency: Defense Academic Research Support Program, 1992), 98.

completely amenable to accepting participation in the existing political process. Others may challenge the very legitimacy of the state system and campaign for its abolishment in its present form, to be replaced by their understanding of a proper Islamic state as embodied in sources such as the Quran, hadiths and sharia.

Among the groups which fall under the rubric of Islam, it is possible to make five distinctions. These distinctions become useful in avoiding the mistake of labeling all politically and socially active Islamic entities as Islamic fundamentalists. First, there is state Islam, such as the present system of government in Saudi Arabia. The puritanical Wahhabism of Saudi Arabia is strict and does condone behavior antithetical to generally accepted Western values, such as polygyny. State Islam, however, is not necessarily a threat, nor an irreconciliable barrier to friendly relations with the West.

Next, there is the high ulama, or those among the religious learned who have studied Islam in the structured theological institutions of the Islamic World, such as Al-Azhar University. Not withstanding the occasional exceptions, this class of pious Muslims, particularly of the Sunni sect, has been guided traditionally to support the state and to avoid politics, as taught by the great scholar of his time, Al Ghazzali, (1058-1111).[15]

A third distinction under the greater rubric of Islam involves Islamic societies. Many of these societies appear most interested in improving local living conditions. Their actions often involve the building of clinics and schools. A prime example is the mainstream element of the Muslim Brotherhood of Egypt.

Fourth, there are popular Islamic movements, such as the National Salvation Front in Algeria. Turkey's fundamentalist political parties would also fall into this category. Many of these popular movements desire to reform the state, often by working within the political boundaries. However, it is often unclear from their political platforms, if they would be willing to eventually relinquish power when necessary, as dictated in a democratic system, and respect the rights of non-Muslims once in control.

Finally, there is the fifth group of fundamentalists, which should be of concern to the West. These are the militants feared in Western minds for their notorious, apparently wanton acts of violence. Among the more notable actions associated with these militants are the

---

[15]Professor Ralph Magnus, NS 3320, Naval Postgraduate School, 9 Mar 93.

9

assassination of Anwar Sadat, the bombing of the U.S. Marine barracks in Lebanon, and, most recently, the murders outside of the headquarters of the Central Intelligence Agency, and the bombing of the World Trade Center building in New York. The various entities which conduct or support these acts justify their violence through unorthodox, often twisted interpretations of Islam. These are unquestionably the true Islamic fundamentalists which threaten U.S. interests.

Unfortunately, the often questionable long-term intentions of the populist element and the militant sect are also the most noticeable aspects of the wider, generally peaceful revival occurring within Islam. These two aspects are mistakenly symbolic in the West of much of what this religion and its resurgence represent. As the evidence alleged to purport a strong fundamentalist movement in Turkey, or elsewhere in the Muslim World is presented, these important distinctions should be applied to separate the true fundamentalist elements of concern, from those groups associated with Islam which are neither a political threat to the indigenous government, nor threatening from a Western perspective.

B. THE ARGUMENTS FOR AN ISLAMIC THREAT IN TURKEY

Among the strongest evidence being touted today that Islamic sentiments are on the rise in Turkey are the

successes of Islamic parties in local and national
elections. Recently, these successes can be divided
into two periods. The first period involved the achievements
of the former ruling Motherland Party (Anavatan Partisi or
ANAP) of Turgut Ozal, and his successor Yildirim Akbulut.[16]
During their reigns as Prime Minister, in which ANAP had a
commanding control of the Grand National Assembly,[17] they
implemented certain Islamic practices and appointed numerous
politicians with Islamic leanings to key positions
throughout the various ministries of the Turkish
bureaucracy. This period of Islamic advancement began with
ANAP's ascendancy in 1983, and Ozal's selection as Prime
Minister.[18] It ended with ANAP's failure to maintain
control of the Grand National Assembly and the Prime
Minister's post in the 20 October 1991 elections.[19]

---

[16]Akbulut replaced Ozal as Prime Minister when Ozal was elected
President in November 1989, through his party's control of
parliament. Barchard, 208.

[17]The Grand National Assembly is the legislative body of
Turkey. It consists of 450 deputies who are elected every five
years. Paul M. Pitman III, ed., Turkey: A Country Study 4th ed.,
(Washington, D.C.: Government Priting Office, 1988), 248.

[18]Feroz Ahmad, "Politics and Islam in Modern Turkey," Middle
Eastern Studies, Vol. 27, No. 1, (Jan 1991), 18.

[19]The locus of power in the Turkish Government is the Prime
Minister's post. This position belongs to the head of the ruling
party of the Grand National Assembly. The post is presently held by
Suleyman Demirel of the ruling True Path Party. The post of
President, which is subservient in power to the Prime Minister, was

It is interesting to note that during Ozal's tenure as Prime Minister, he was considered by the U.S. as a staunch ally and beacon of stability in a region troubled by Islamic activism and aggressive dictators. One need only reflect on the numerous personal phone calls, visits, and photo opportunities between him and former Presidents Reagan and Bush, and even a visit to Turkey by Bush, to understand that, up to his death, Ozal was a close ally of the U.S. And yet, this close alliance between the U.S. and Ozal seems to stand in stark contrast to his background and the makeup of the ANAP party.

To discuss ANAP and its connection with Islamic activism, the origins of this party must be briefly reviewed. On 12 September 1980, the Turkish General Staff stepped in to take control of a quickly disintegrating Turkey. For almost the entire previous ten years political violence had run rampant in Turkey between left and right wing students and terrorist organizations. Between 1976 and 1980, political violence resulted in the deaths of an estimated 4,500 Turks.[20] After a severe clamping down by the military on political activities, which included the arrest

---

held by Turgut Ozal until his death in April 1993.

[20]Sabri Sayari and Bruce Hoffman, Urbanization and Insurgency: The Turkish Case, 1976-1980 (Santa Montica, CA: RAND, 1991), 10.

of various political leaders, the junta started to relinquish power in April 1983. At this time, civilian political parties were allowed to partially resume their activities. Still, a clause in the new 1982 constitution, written by the junta, allowed this group to bar certain parties and candidates from returning to politics.[21] In essence, many of the parties and leaders dominant during the unrest of the 1970's were not allowed to return to the fray of Turkish politics.[22] New political parties were therefore created in order to participate in future elections. One of these parties was the Motherland Party (ANAP), founded in May 1983, by Turgut Ozal.[23] How much different these new political parties are from those of the 1970's is a matter open to debate. ANAP is itself a coalition of several elements from the predominant parties of the pre-coup era.[24] Among the important elements in ANAP were members of the "Islamic fundamentalist" National Salvation Party (Milli

---

[21]Pitman, 261.

[22]Ibid., 261.

[23]Ibid., 268.

[24]Ibid.

Selamet Partisi or MSP).[25] Established in 1973, the MSP was one of the first Islamic parties in Turkey.[26]

Ozal was obviously the champion of free market philosophy and Western values in Turkish politics. Why then, would the National Salvation Party align itself with Turgut Ozal's ANAP party? They aligned themselves with Ozal because, among the limited political parties and figures allowed to participate when civilian politics resumed in the early 1980's, he was the only candidate with credentials to attract fundamentalist supporters, as well as more moderate elements of Turkish society. He had actually run for a parliament seat in 1977 as a National Salvation Party candidate.[27] Furthermore, Ozal is, "the son of a highly pious family of Nakishibendi (or Naqshabandi) dervishes from the eastern Anatolian town of Malatya."[28] This dervish order played an important role in opposing secularism in Turkey under Ataturk in the 1920's and 1930's. One Nakishibendi Sheykh, Sheykh Said, was instrumental in using Islam as the medium for instigating a Kurdish revolt in

---

[25]Ibid., 268, 438.

[26]Ahmad, 13.

[27]Ibid.

[28]Barchard, 109. President Ozal actually told the visiting Nakishibendi head of Central Asia that he was also from that order. Olcott, 125.

14

1925. This revolt was eventually declared a jihad by the Sheykh.[29] Another dervish of this order, Dervish Mehmed, instigated a revolt in a town near Izmir in 1930, declared that he was the Mahdi and called for a restoration of the sharia and caliphate.[30]

As an important part of the ruling ANAP coalition, National Salvation Party members under Ozal were in an obvious position to influence government policies. The results of this influence amounted to the victories of the first period of Islamic successes alluded to earlier. An example of these victories included the following:

> The 1990 budget increases the spending of the Office of the President of Religious Affairs, which looks after the clergy of Turkey's Sunni mosques, by 237 per cent, pushing it ahead of several fully-fledged ministries. The increase, it is said, is to enable more personnel to be hired. For the first time, the Office is demanding the right to be cut free from the state and made into an autonomous body....

> ...Around the same time there was a nation-wide campaign, supported by several Cabinet Ministers and not opposed to Mr Akbulut, to convert the Museum of St Sophia, the sixth-century basilica built by Emperor Justinian and one of Turkey's premier historic monuments and tourist attractions into a mosque. This appeared to be a systematic bid to reverse Ataturk's secularizing reforms of the 1930's.[31]

---

[29]Ahmad, 6-7.

[30]Ibid., 7.

[31]Barchard, 109.

In addition, the "conservative" or "Holy Alliance"[32] element of ANAP was also successful in passing a bill which allowed female students in the universities to wear the Islamic headdress.[33] The headdress, "turban" or bas ortusu (headscarf), as it is known in Turkey, has been regarded as one of the most visible and controversial symbols of growing Islamic activism in the country.[34] To some secular Turks, the turban has been equated to veiling.

Among the reforms spearheaded in the early years of the Turkish Republic by Ataturk, a concerted effort was made to change the dress of both males and females. Laws were therefore passed to enforce the wear of European style clothing.[35] This was just one of many reforms inspired by Mustafa Kemal, later known as "Ataturk," in an effort to, "'disestablish' Islam in Turkey," and "to limit its powers

---

[32]These are two terms used by fellow ANAP members in describing the Islamic activists in their coalition. "Yilmaz Fires Fundamentalists from Key Posts," Nokta, Foreign Broadcast Information Service, Western Europe, (Hereafter "FBIS"), 28 Jul 91.

[33]"Derya Sazak, 'Toward Polarization,' Paper Views Islamic, Secular Polarizations," Milliyet, FBIS, 7 Nov 1990.

[34]For an excellent discussion on the history and symbolism of the "headscarf dispute" read, Emelie A. Olson, "Muslim Identity and Secularism in Contemporary Turkey: "The Headscarf Dispute," Anthropological Quarterly, Vol. 58, No. 4, (1985), 161-171.

[35]Ibid., 164.

on matters of belief and worship."[36] Elimination of the man's fez is rather well known, but the woman's veil and carsaf, "a bedsheet-like overgarment covering a woman's head and body," were also attacked as "backward," and against the principles of the reform minded Ataturk.[37]

In 1984, this issue gained renewed attention when Dr. Docent Koru, a university professor, became embroiled in a battle with her school's staff over her insistence to wear a headscarf while teaching.[38] By 1989, demonstrations in favor of the wear of the headscarf led some to speculate this was the beginning of a mass Islamic movement with the potential to challenge, "the very foundation of the Kemalist state."[39]

The bill which eventually supported the wear of the headscarf resulted from a "clandestine" provision put forth by the budget committee of the Grand National Assembly, under the control of ANAP at the time.[40]

---

[36]Bernard Lewis, The Emergence of Modern Turkey, (New York: Oxford University Press, 1968), In Olson, 164.

[37]Olson, 164.

[38]Ibid., 161.

[39]Philip Robins, Turkey and the Middle East, (New York: Council on Foreign Relations Press, 1991), 43.

[40]FBIS, 7 Nov 1990.

Furthermore, this same conservative faction of ANAP worked unsuccessfully to pass a bill through parliament which would have brought "practical" religious lessons into the secular school system.[41]

Another apparent Islamic victory under Ozal was the signing of a decree regarding "the foundation of special finance houses."[42] These special finance houses were actually references to Islamic banks. This decree provided these banks with special privileges over conventional Turkish banks in the amount of money they were required to maintain in the reserve of Turkey's central bank.[43]

Symbolic as these achievements and attempts were, the real success for the Islamic wing of ANAP is not to be found in these piecemeal accomplishments. Instead, these moves were merely symptomatic of the true power gained by the Islamic members of the ANAP coalition through their appointments to key positions throughout the numerous ministries of the government. These appointments were certainly necessary if Ozal was to keep the MSP element in

---

[41]Ibid.

[42]Clement Henry Moore, "Islamic Banks and Competitive Politics in the Arab World and Turkey," Middle East Journal, Vol. 44, No. 2 (Spring 1990), 247.

[43]Ibid., 247

the ANAP coalition, and involved positions in all the important ministries, to include the security apparatus.

The political assignment of Islamic activists in the Turkish National Police (Genel Emniyet Mudurlugu or GEM)[44] organization is particularly useful in demonstrating the extent of these appointments and the power the Islamic wing of ANAP had garnered.[45] A small listing of just some GEM officials considered to be "fundamentalists" included the following:

> ...the director general of security (the head of the
> GEM); his deputy, Mr. Muharrem; the head of Interpol;
> the head of civilian intelligence, Mr Ali Gokcimen; the
> dean of the Police Academy and his aides, and the heads
> of the police schools since 6 November 1983 in terms of
> security, police work and interior affairs.[46]

These Islamic activists appointed to the top bureaucratic positions were naturally influential. High ranking members in the GEM felt compelled out of fear of losing their jobs or being transferred to dangerous locations in Eastern Turkey to attend Friday prayer services

---

[44]Genel Emniyet Mudurlugu is translated to General Directorate of Security. It may also be referred to as the the Turkish National Police.

[45]The Turkish National Police (TNP) is responsible for all criminal activity, including terrorism, in the urban areas of Turkey. Besides the Jandarma, which fall under the military for all practical purposes, the TNP is the only police organization in the country.

[46]"Prosperity Member Scores ANAP for 'Purges,'" Nokta, FBIS, 28 Jul 91.

at the mosque because their new bosses were "fundamentalists." Fundamentalist control of the top and middle management positions of the GEM were believed so complete and pervasive, that some police officers believed these members hindered and even sabotaged police efforts to control Islamic fundamentalist terrorist groups. One security chief in Istanbul is said to have appointed graduates of "imam and preacher schools" to 21 of 22 faculty positions in the Istanbul Police Academy.[47]

This assessment of fundamentalist infiltration into the GEM and other organizations was also a view held by the Turkish National Intelligence Organization (Milli Istihbarat Teskilati or MIT).[48] In fact, because of Islamic appointments to the General Directorate of Security, MIT distrust became so great that a rift occurred between the two organizations. This rift was so serious that, "For a long time, MIT refused to pass on any serious information to the security directorate."[49] By comparison, in the U.S. this would be tantamount to having the CIA refuse to work with the FBI.

---

[47]FBIS, 28 Jul 91.

[48]MIT is similar to the U.S. Central Intelligence Agency, but also has a domestic responsibility for gathering intelligence against organizations working against the state.

[49]FBIS, 28 Jul 91.

Eventually, the issue of fundamentalist infiltration into all ranks and ministries of the government came to a head in November 1990, when Lieutenant General Teoman Koman, Under-Secretary of MIT, briefed the new Prime Minister Yildirim Akbulut, of the threat. In the words of the General Koman, "religious fanaticism has even infiltrated the ranks of police units and is trying to devour the state."[50]

Akbulut was obviously not pleased by the Koman's remarks as it was his own ANAP party which was responsible for their entry into the government. However, the powerful Turkish General Staff, which had instigated the coup of 12 September 1980, and which believes it has the nation's special trust for upholding the values of Ataturk against all enemies, external or internal, backed the general and his organization's message. Clearly, the military was sending a veiled threat to the Prime Minister that the advancement of Islamic, anti-secular and thus anti-Ataturk values, had gone too far.

The result of the MIT warning backed by the military was a massive purge begun in July 1991, by the mainstream element in ANAP. Through all the ministries of government those officials thought to be Islamic fundamentalists were

---

[50]"NIO Briefs Government on Religious Fanaticism," Gunaydin, FBIS, 10 Nov 90.

swept out of office and replaced by secular reformers. One newspaper published a partial "purge list" of thirty top officials in ministries ranging from the Ministry of Justice, State Planning, Merchant Marine and Tanker Administration, to Public Housing, Labor and Tourism.[51] One anonymous minister summarized the problem of Islamic activists in government positions and the purge this way:

> I think that when this operation is completed the total number [of people replaced] will be in the thousands. Government agencies have been taken over to such an extent that, just as in the security organizations, people who begin preparing for their Friday prayers hours earlier, who keep copies of the Koran and cult books in their desk drawers and who wear silver rings are everywhere. People have been appointed to desks and positions not on the basis of their competence, but on the strength of their faith.[52]

In the ANAP itself, the result was a party congress which called for the replacement in September 1991, of Prime Minister Akbulut by the more acceptable Mesut Yilmaz, who conducted the purges with vigor.[53] Prior to this purge of Islamic activists in government positions, Prime Minister Akbulut is said to have been powerless to act against the rise of the Islamic front. His hands were tied because he was attempting to maintain their fading support of the

---

[51]"New Government's 'Purge List' Detailed," Nokta, FBIS, 28 Jul 91.

[52]FBIS, 28 Jul 91.

[53]Ibid.

ruling ANAP coalition.[54] This crisis of sorts for ANAP
occurred as the Islamic wing of ANAP started to abandon its
coalition partner for support of the more outwardly Islamic
party, the Prosperity Party (Refah Partisi or Welfare or
People's Toil Party).[55]

C. PUTTING THE SIGNS OF TURKEY'S "ISLAMIC THREAT" INTO PERSPECTIVE

Undoubtedly, there have been expressions of Islamic
activism in Turkey during the 1980's and up to the present
time. The infiltration into the government of Islamic
"conservatives" from the "Holy Alliance" wing of Ozal's
Motherland Party, the approval of legislation regarding
Islamic headdresses, Islamic banking, and the increase of
the Religious Ministry's budget, are all seen as evidence of
this movement. Yet, if the political and social evidence
are examined more thoroughly, the case for listing Turkey as
a country under the threatening shadow of radical Islam
begins to unravel. Several symbolic actions during the
Motherland Party's control of the government between 1983-
1991 are examples of actions associated with Islam, but
which are incorrectly construed as proof of Islamic
activisim.

---

[54]Ibid.

[55]Ibid.

A good example of the incorrect association between actions in Turkey related to Islam which could be erroneously construed as evidence of Islamic activism involves the expansion of Islamic banking. It is a logical jump in making the connection from the Quran's rejection of usury and the avoidance of this problem through the methods of Islamic banks, to the conclusion that the expansion of these banks therefore reflects society's desires to return to the purity of the Quran. However, while Islamic Banks were established by decree and given certain privileges soon after Ozal took office in 1983, the impetus for these actions were hardly Islamic.

Professor Clement Henry Moore has suggested several reasons for Ozal's actions. None of the explanations which follow are related to the cause of advancing Islam over secular values. For instance, one justification for Ozal's support of these banks is graft. Turgut Ozal's brother, Korkot, who was instrumental in introducing Islamic bankers to his politician brother, stood to profit by the introduction of such banks in Turkey. These banks would help finance oil imports into Turkey, in which Korkut Ozal had a stake.[56] However, as Moore points out, these oil deals came

---

[56]Moore, 248.

about after the banks were already established.[57] This would weaken such an argument.

Another and stronger explanation is purely political. As the leftists in the country had been decimated by the coup of 12 September 1980, the only threat to Ozal's hold on power came from the far-right elements in the country, which include the Islamicists and hard-line nationalists. Ozal therefore stood to profit politically by co-opting the support of the Islamicists away from the far-right parties to his center-right ANAP party.[58] This could be done with symbolic gestures, such as the decree regarding Islamic banking.

Third, as Moore mentions in his conclusions, but which he did not directly recognize as an explanation for Ozal's actions, the entrance of Islamic banks into Turkey makes good business sense. By thrusting the Islamic banks into Turkey's business sector, it would force a badly needed element of competition into the Turkish banking system and other elements of society. Moore feels this competition could help to advance several pro-Western views in Turkey. Specifically, he had the following to say about the utility

---

[57]Ibid.

[58]Ibid., 248.

of Ozal's use of Islamic banks for the purpose of injecting competition into Turkish society:

> ...he may make Turkish financial markets more competitive and also break oligopolistic public-private understandings in other sectors of the economy. Such a transformation might give Turkey the economic base needed to break out of its political cycle of authoritarianism and pluralism toward a more stable form of democracy.[59]

It would obviously be false then to conclude that the expansion of Islamic banks in Turkey in the 1980's was for reasons associated purely with the advancement of Islamic activism.

A similar fallacious argument for the strength of fundamentalist Islamic tendencies in Turkey is presented in the turban issue. This symbol is regarded by Turkish university academics, where the turban is most visible and vehemently protested, as a "symbol of certain beliefs and against secularism."[60] Anakara's Hacettepe University medical faculty were so opposed to the wearing of the turban that they went as far as boycotting classes and placing advertisements in daily newspapers in protest.[61] Yet, it has not been established that the turban is solely symbolic

---

[59]Ibid., 254-255.

[60]"University Concerned Over Headgear Liberalization," Anatolia, FBIS, 9 Nov 1990.

[61]Ibid.

of fundamentalist tendencies. The turban parallels veiling,
and of course, there are numerous reasons for veiling
besides its symbolic display of belief in Islamic activism.
Reasons for veiling include the following:

> Interpretation of a passage in the Quran regarding
> the statement that, "women should cover their
> ornaments"; as protection from the undesired advances
> of men; in order to be modest and protect their
> reputation; as a form of youthful rebellion against
> parents or society regarded as secular (going against
> the norms of society); as an expression they will not
> compete in a society which values outward beauty; as a
> result of poverty; from coercion by others who require
> veiling; in deference to their men; and finally as a
> political statement.[62]

How can the argument be made then that the headscarf in
Turkey is only related to Islamic activism?

Feroz Ahmad has suggested two reasons why women in
Turkey wear the turban, neither of which are an expression
of fundamentalist Islam. The first explanation regards the
use of the turban as a symbol of protest against the "Higher
Education Law" of 1983.[63] This law, "ended university
autonomy and treated students like children by legislating a
dress code."[64] This is the same interpretation of this
issue expounded by the rector of Aegean University, where

---

[62]Professor Glenn Robinson, NS 4300 discussion, 20 Jan 93,
Naval Postgraduate School.

[63]Ahmad, 18.

[64]Ibid.

Dr. Koru taught, when he said, "Docent Koru talks about freedom of religion and conscience, but...the subject is related only to the Dress Regulation.[65]

The second reason for the wear of the turban is even more interesting and completely antithetical to the notion this symbol is fundamentalist in nature. Ahmad had the following to say:

> Far from being Islamists in the traditional mould, many in the movement who supported the headscarf campaign were 'Islamic feminists' who wanted to use Islam to liberate themselves from the oppression of their patriarchial society. This was an urban phenomenon amongst women who are sufficiently 'traditional' to describe themselves as primarily Muslim, but who wanted to play an active role in society because they either wanted to work in order to fulfill themselves or had to work because of economic necessity. It was also a revolt against the drudgery of housework, especially onerous in Turkey.[66]

In this case, Islam is being used as support for equality of the sexes, a very modern and pro-Western value. This understanding of the symbolism behind the headscarf is supported by others, such as ANAP deputy Turkan Arikan, who spoke of, "relationships between this matter and women's rights and religious attitudes."[67]

---

[65]Olson, 162.

[66]Ahmad, 18.

[67]Olson, 162.

Cultural anthropologist, Emelie Olson's work, which
began many years prior to the sensationalism of the
"headscarf dispute," also suggests that equating the
headscarf to Islamic fundamentalism is a gross
oversimplification. For instance, her observations between
1964 and 1984 led her to conclude that, "outside of
religious contexts, wearing either the headkerchief or the
'babushka,' was more 'conventional' than 'Muslim.'"[68] The
"babushka" is a Western style scarf knotted under the
chin.[69]

Furthermore, in reference to the specific question of
the significance of the turban after 1984, when the issue
was rekindled by Professor Koru's actions, Dr. Olson wrote
the following:

> These incidents of July, 1984, which I have
> referred to as the "headscarf disupte," should be
> interpreted as recent skirmishes in a long-term
> conflict between two major ideological systems in modern
> Turkey, one which has been built into the very fabric
> of Turkey's political, social, economic, and cultural
> systems since before the founding of the Republic.
> Although there are several strands to this conflict,
> and the two poles vary according to such factors as the
> incident, the locale, the participants, or the
> commentators, in broad terms it is between two opposing
> sets of orientation. As it relates to the present
> dispute, perhaps the two most important variants of the
> "two sides" in the ideological conflict are 1) Turkish

---

[68]Ibid., 165.

[69]Ibid.

"nationalism" versus Muslim identity and 2) secularism (laicism) versus an "Islamic society."

This ideological conflict is more dialectical than merely oppositional. Over the last 150 years or so, Turkish realizations of "nationalism versus "Muslim identity" and of "secularism" versus an "Islamic society," respectively, have evolved not in isolation but in interaction with each other.[70]

Dr. Olson goes on to make another very crucial point which is not only applicable to the specific issue of the headscarf, or turban, but to the larger issue of how to interpret the aims and strength of Islamic resurgence in Turkey in general. She wrote the following:

...contemporary Turkish interpretations of "secularism" and "Islamic Society" can lead to complicated and unpredictable results. First, "secularism" may mean 1) being a fervent follower of "Ataturk's" ideologies, 2) practicing Islam as a private citizen in a secular state, or 3) both. Proponents of an "Islamic society" vary greatly in their definitions of such a society and the degree to which they would impose "Islamic" practices on the populace. Thus, within this context, it is very significant that Prof. Koru defends her wearing of the headscarf while teaching by arguing to her "constitutional rights" rather than by appealing to Muslim authority.[71]

This important insight highlights the point made earlier of the necessity to distinguish between social and political Islamic resurgence, and between threatening and non-threating elements of this phenonmenon. Clearly then, while the headscarf issue in Turkey is tied to Islam, this is not

---

[70]Ibid.

[71]Ibid., 167.

evidence that the movement is related strictly to Islamic fundamentalism. As discussed above, the headscarf also involves matters of women's rights, traditional dress, reaction to the authority embodied in a dress code, the societal struggle to define "secularism" versus "Islamic society," and the individual struggle to define Turkish "nationalism" and "Muslim identity."

As for the "clandestine" bill which reversed previous laws on the wear of the turban, it should be accepted as a positive move by ANAP which defused the incident. As Dr. Philip Robins concluded, "The fact that the demonstrations over the turban affairs, which in any case never attracted mass participation, evaporated after the resolution of the incident appears to have gone unnoticed."[72]

The issues of Islamic banking and the turban were allegedly symbolic of rising Islamic sentiments. At best, these have been shown to be inconclusive evidence of increasing Islamic activism in Turkey. However, the real success of the Islamic activists was suggested to have been with the power and influence they received as part of Turgut Ozal's Motherland Party coalition. How can their power in this coalition, which allowed them to staff the numerous ministries of the government with personnel friendly to

---

[72]Robins, 43.

their cause, be explained? The answer is not to be found in suggesting that Ozal or the main element of the Motherland Party are Islamic activists. Regardless of Ozal's Nakishibendi heritage or former association with the National Salvation Party, his pro-Western policies for the economic development of Turkey, support of Turkey's application for entry into the European Economic Community, and staunch support of the U.S. and West, are what truly defined his politics.[73] These are the reasons he was so endeared to Presidents Reagan and Bush. Instead, the rationale for Ozal's incorporation of the Islamicists into his ruling coalition rests with the more practical explanation of party politics.

In 1980, when the military cracked down on the extremists and political parties in the country, they were particularly harsh on the extreme left and right-wings of the political spectrum. By 1983, when civilian politics were resumed, only three parties were allowed by the generals to compete. These were Ozal's "moderately right-of-center" Motherland Party, and two parties led by generals, one of

---

[73]One need only review Ozal's actions in supporting the U.S. led war in the Gulf to observe his pro-Western values. These Actions included his unpopular decisions to allow U.S. aircraft to fly missions from Turkish bases and support of Operation Provide Comfort to assist the Kurds in Iraq.

which was right-of-center, and the other left-of-center.[74]

The spectrum of civilian political expression in Turkey was therefore very much truncated compared with previous elections. Ozal's party claimed to represent all the parties which had been prevented from participating in the elections. This included the National Salvation Party, which consequently lent its support to the Motherland Party.[75] Ozal's party easily won a majority 211 out of 400 seats in the parliament.[76] It seems apparent now that the cost to Ozal of accepting the National Salvation Party's support were the appointments of some personnel friendly to their Islamic platform. As restrictions were relaxed on political parties, the National Salvation Party, reemerged as the Prosperity Party, still under Necmettin Erbakan. As they were allowed once again to participate in parliamentary elections, Ozal and later Yildirim Akbulut were forced to grant further concessions to the "conservative" element of ANAP to keep them from defecting to Erbakan. Therefore, it must be concluded that Ozal's incorporation of the "Holy

---

[74]Jacob M. Landau, "Democratic Framework and Military Control," in Ideology and Power in the Middle East: Studies in honor of George Lenczowski, ed. Peter J. Chelkowski and Robert J. Pranger (Durham, N.C.: Duke University Press, 1988), 318.

[75]Ahmad, 18.

[76]Monthly Statistics of Foreign Trade, Economic and Statistics Department of the OECD, June 1992, 928.

Alliance" element into the Motherland Party and the cost of passing symbolic legislation and appointing Islamic friendly personnel to the ministries is not based on the capture of the parliament or Prime Minister's post by Islamic activists. Rather, this was simply the cost of doing business in a multiparty system in which opposing parties were competing for support.

II. FOCUSING ON THE "ISLAMIC THREAT" THROUGH THE ELECTORAL PROCESS

Dr. Philip Robins, Head of the Middle East Programme at the Royal Institute of International Affairs, has made an interesting observation worth quoting at length. He said the following:

> Since the Iranian revolution, Western strategists have been preoccupied by the "Islamic Threat", especially in traditionally friendly Muslim states. Contemporary analysts are forever being urged to consider whether such states are likely to "go Muslim". Since the late 1980's, this is a question which had been asked with greater urgency in relation to Turkey. It has become fashionable once more to speak of Turkey as being increasingly fundamentalist and hence closer to becoming unstable.[77]

The accuracy of this statement is evident when considering stories in the Western press, some of which have been previously mentioned, which proclaim the dangers of an inherently anti-Western, political, and resurgent Islam.

As Robins goes on to suggest, Islamicist movements may challenge an existing government in three distinct ways. First, he describes, "the direct challenge to the prevailing regime, unmediated by constitutional propriety and possibly

---

[77]Philip Robins, Turkey and the Middle East, New York: Council on Foreign Relations Press, 1991), 43.

incorporating the use of political violence."[78] Second, he speaks of the Islamic threat to a government through participation and victory in that state's electoral process.[79] Hidden in this threat is the nefarious implication that any Islamic party gaining the reigns of government through the democratic process, would renounce such means once in power and attempt to establish the permanency of their rule. And third, Robins describes the "indirect influence" Islamicists can exert upon policy.[80]

With regard to applying these three manifestations of the alleged Islamicist threat to Turkey, I must dismiss the first out of hand for insufficient evidence. Already mentioned in this regard is the issue of the turban, which was at one time considered by some to be symbolic of the beginning of a mass Islamic movement. This movement neither lasted very long once its legality was not in question, nor as the work of Dr. Olson and others have shown, is the turban worn strictly for reasons associated with Islamic activism.

The inability of fundamentalists, as well as nationalists, to gather more than 10,000 people in a rally

---

[78]Ibid.

[79]Ibid., 44.

[80]Ibid., 45.

at Taksim Square in Istanbul in February of 1993, for the
purpose of showing solidarity for the Muslims of
Bosnia-Hercegovina, further detracts from any argument based
on the "direct threat."[81] Editorialist Ilnur Cevik of the
Turkish Daily News analyzed this rally well when he wrote
the following:

> As politicians like Suleyman Demirel and Bulent
> Ecevit have managed to pack more than 100,000 people
> into Taksim Square in past political rallies, what
> happened at Taksim on Saturday was really a "nonevent"
> as it hardly demonstrated massive Turkish public
> support for a cause...
>
> ...Unlike the outcome of Saturday's rally, the
> masses in Turkey are extremely sensitive to what is
> going on in Bosnia against the Muslims and is angry
> with the Serbs. Yet the public in Turkey refuses to be
> a part of any extremist act.[82]

It would appear then that even with a genuinely popular
cause with which to unite the country, the fundamentalists
are ineffective at mobilizing the Turkish population behind
their platform. They therefore can not realistically be
considered a "direct threat" to the Turkish state.

The threat of "indirect influence" by the Islamicists
must also be negated. It should instead be regarded as
a healthy sign, not a threat, that Turkey's much maligned
democracy allows the Islamicists to have a legitimate outlet

---

[81]"Editorial Says Ozal 'Humiliated' at Istanbul Rally," Turkish
Daily News, FBIS, 15 Feb 93.

[82]Ibid.

for influencing government. Furthermore, as mentioned earlier, and to be discussed in greater detail later, Turkish democracy has already survived rather large degrees of indirect Islamic Influence during the 1970's and 1980's.

This brings us to Robins' second description of the manifestation by which the Islamicists may threaten Turkey-through the electoral process. The alleged growth of Islamic electoral strength in Turkey is, incidently, probably the most popular evidence in the Western press of Islamic resurgence in Turkey.

Since the 20 Oct 1991 Grand National Assembly elections, the fundamentalist Prosperity Party (Refah Partisi, also translated from Turkish into the People's Toiling Party or Welfare Party), has become very fashionable evidence for some Western pundits and elements of the media which insist on listing Turkey in the category of countries expected to "go Muslim." In this section, I will present evidence that Turkey is not threatened through the electoral process by the Islamic fundamentalists, as embodied in the Prosperity Party and its predecessor the National Salvation Party (Milli Selamet Partisi). This will be done by initially examining the real "success" of the Prosperity Party in the 20 Oct 1991 elections results.

Additionally, as foreign policy is often the result of acting on worst case scenarios, I will also examine the obstacles in Turkish society which would militate the ability of the Prosperity Party to amount to anything more than a junior coalition partner in any near-term government. And, in the hypothetical case that the Prosperity Party were to become a member of a coalition government in the near future, I will likewise discuss the internal checks which would prevent these Islamicists from taking Turkey down a "Muslim path." First, however, it is necessary to briefly discuss the history of the Prosperity Party and what it represents.

A. WHAT IS THE PROSPERITY PARTY?

On 20 October 91, general elections where held throughout Turkey. In a massive show of voter participation the Motherland Party (Anavatan Partisi, or ANAP) of the late President Turgut Ozal and Prime Minister Mesut Yilmaz was defeated and relegated to a secondary standing in the polls for the first time since 1983.[83] The winner was Suleyman

---

[83]Voter participation amounted to 83.92 percent of the eligible 29,978,837, registered voters. This high turnout may have been partially the result of the desire to see a new government. However, the levying of a 50,000 Turkish Lira fine (approximately $10.00) for not voting cannot be discounted. "Elections Held 20 Oct; Nonvoters to Face Fines." Ankara Turkiye Radyolari Network, FBIS, 20 Oct 91.

Demirel's center-right, True Path Party (Dogru Yol Partisi),
which quickly moved to form a coalition government with
Erdal Inonu's left-of-center Social Democratic Populists
Party (Sosyal Demokrat Halkci Parti).[84] This gave Demirel's
coalition 262 seats in the 450 seat Grand National Assembly.

The real surprise of the elections though was the
success of Necmettin Erbakan's Islamic fundamentalist
Prosperity Party which received almost 17 percent of the
vote and 52 parliament seats. This was a dramatic increase
from May of 1991, only six months before the election, when
this Islamic party had just ten seats in parliament.The
distribution of parliament seats among the various parties
is displayed on Tables 1 and 2, located in Appendix A, page
116.

This was also an increase over their support during the
1973 and 1977 elections, when they received just 11.8 and
8.6 percent of the vote, and 48 and 24 parliament seats,
respectively. The 1973 and 1975 election results are
displayed on Table 3, located in Appendix B, page 117

This dramatic jump was reasoned by some to represent the
resurgence of Islamic fundamentalism in Turkey. Shortly
after the initial election results were released, party

---

[84]Sam Cohen, "New Turkish Signals End of Era," Christian Science Monitor, 21 Nov 91.

leader Erbakan had the following to say about his party's

showing:

> Like a volcano, the Prosperity Party shattered all the obstacles and hurdles which were placed in front of it. It is marching to the top...As we have always wished, these elections will be Turkey's salvation. This is what we believe in. As you can see, the other parties remained stagnant or even regressed. Only the Prosperity Party took a great leap forward. It increased its previous percentage of votes by 300 percent, an unprecedented phenomenon in Turkey or any other country.[85]

The Prosperity Party is one of the many political organizations which were formed in 1983, following the partial return of civilian politics from military controls. Like ANAP and others, the Prosperity Party is a continuation of political groups outlawed following the 12 September 1980 coup. It is the Islamic activist National Salvation Party (Milli Selamet Partisi) which is the basis of this latest Islamic party.[86] Necmettin Erbakan, the Prosperity Party leader, also led the old National Salvation Party.[87] It is his brand of Islamic activism and the spectacular jump his party made in the 20 Oct 1991, elections which have resulted

---

[85]"Prosperity Party Leader," Ankara Turkiye Radyolari Network, FBIS, 21 Oct 91.

[86]Paul M. Pitman III, ed., Turkey: A Country Study 4th ed., (Washington, D.C.: Government Printing Office, 1988), 273.

[87]Ibid., 273.

in many Westerners fortelling the rise of Islamic sentiments in Turkey. What exactly is this party espousing?

In broad terms, the Prosperity Party's goals, as espoused by Erbakan, appear to be the establishment of government under the sovereignty of God. Government would therefore play a "coordinating role" between God and society.[88] This coordinating role would be accomplished through the use of the Quran. As far back as 1972, when Erbakan was leader of the National Salvation Party, the precursor to the Prosperity Party, he had the following to say about this matter:

> It was also asserted that God ordered us to rule according to the Holy Book, not our own judgement. If mankind could be ruled according to votes, men would not need revelation. In societies where affairs are run according to the votes of ordinary people, Islam degenerates. Democracy is a Western plot to rule ignorant people according to Western and Christian ways. It is a victory of Christianity over Islam.[89]

Besides hinting at how the Prosperity Party would derive its sovereignty under God, this statement also raises troubling questions about Erbakan's true commitment to the democratic process in Turkey.[90] Would Erbakan, in fact,

---

[88]"Religious Party Outlines Economic Model," Cumhuriyet, FBIS, 11 Oct 91.

[89]Feroz Ahmad, "Politics and Islam in Modern Turkey," Middle Eastern Studies, Vol. 27, No. 1, (Jan 1991), 15.

[90]Ibid.

operate within the constraints of a democratic government if he were to gain a majority in the assembly? Or, as many people fear, would his Islamic organization, and others throughout the Middle East, only work within democratic boundaries until they had achieved supremacy in the country, with no intent of ever relinquishing power?

According to Necmettin Erbakan, the Turkish Republic's economic system under Prosperity Party leadership would also be drastically altered. Sounding very much like the famous Egyptian Islamic ideologue Sayyid Qutb, as well as as echoing what might be considered communist dogma, Erbakan believes that Western economic models have led to a "system of slavery" resulting in an unjust society.[91] In Erbakan's own words, "Capitalism is oppressing and exploiting the ordinary workers and laborers."[92] Capitalism, however, is not the only instigator of this unjust society. Western imperialism as well as Zionism are also singled out as the "pincers" crushing Turkey and other Muslim nations.[93] This combination of Zionism, Western imperialism, and an

---

[91]FBIS, 11 Oct 91.

[92]Ibid.

[93]Ibid.

"interest-based capitalist system," in Erbakan's view,
results in:[94]

> oppressing millions of people by condemning them to
> high prices, hunger, poverty, unemployment and
> backwardness and is turning over their rights unjustly
> to imperialism, world Zionism and a happy minority that
> is collaborating with them.[95]

It is not exactly clear how the Prosperity Party will
overcome these injustices and create a model society, but
Erbakan has alluded to a few vague notions.

First, he definitely would turn away from Western
economic entanglements, such as the Economic Community, and
turn instead towards Muslim cooperation. The ultimate goal
of this first point would be the establishment of a common
Muslim economic market.[96]

Second, he would abolish the "five viruses of
interest-based capitalism" which hold Turkey back
from prosperity.[97] These five viruses are interest, unjust
taxation, printing money, exchange rates, and credit.[98]

Third, Erbakan would concentrate on building up the
heavy industry of Turkey, in what appears to a be a

---

[94]Ibid.

[95]Ibid.

[96]Ibid.

[97]Ibid.

[98]Ibid.

repetition of the old Import Substitution Industrialization model.[99]

Fourth, Erbakan speaks of injecting morals into economics through concepts such as "solidarity groups," which would act like guilds, and "moral groups" which would approve business loans and various economic transactions based on an applicant's moral character.[100]

In addition to castigating Turkey's economic patterns, Erbakan also has espoused a very personal message. Like other Islamic idealogues, he is quick to make use of the alienation and cognitive dissonance many Turks probably feel from the scope and pace of Western influences in their society.[101] As early as 1969, when Erbakan ran for a seat in the Grand National Assembly as an independent member of parliament from Konya, he said the following:[102]

> Thus the European, by making us copy him blindly and without any understanding, trapped us in this monkey's cage and, as a result, forced us to abandon our personality and nobility. That is to say, he was successful in this because he used agents recruited from within, who felt (inferior and) disgusted with themselves, bringing to his knees the Turk who for

---

[99]"Religious Leader on Tax, Foreign Investment," Panorama, FBIS, 17 Nov 91.

[100]FBIS, 11 Oct 91.

[101]Professor Glen Robinson, NS 4300, Naval Postgraduate School, 24 Feb 93.

[102]Ahmad, 14.

centuries could not be defeated by the crusades and external blows.[103]

This message of alienation is particularly powerful as it is highlighted against the backdrop of Turkey's glorious martial history, of which most Turks are very knowledgeable. Furthermore, this message hints at the present, unnatural reversal of dominance between the West and Turkey.

In summing up the essence of Necmettin Erbakan's Prosperity Party, it must be concluded that his message is both of material and moral prosperity, as well as a role for Turkey in leading the Muslim World, reminiscent of Turkey's past. Feroz Ahmad, summed up Erbakan's message this way:

> ...he was promising to create a modern, industrial prosperous Turkey with social justice and democratic rights for all; a Turkey no longer 'enslaved by the West' but one which was independent and played the role of leader in the Muslim world.[104]

B. SUMMING UP THE REAL SUCCESS OF THE PROSPERITY PARTY

On 1 Nov 1991 the Prosperity Party gained 52 seats in the parliament for a total of 62 seats. This would outwardly represent an explosive rise in popularity, as implied by Erbakan's boasting about a "volcano." However, when the election results of the Prosperity Party are examined in

---

[103]Ibid., 14-15.

[104]Ibid.

46

detail, the possibility of this party gaining majority control of the government becomes almost implausible.

As discussed earlier, following the 12 Sept 1980, coup, restrictions were eventually relaxed on political parties. The National Salvation Party, now reformed and renamed as the Prosperity Party, but still under Necmettin Erbakan, was allowed once again to participate in parliamentary elections. The Prosperity Party then successfully challenged Ozal's claim to continue to represent the defunct National Salvation Party, or the Islamic fundamentalists.[105] As ANAP was never sufficiently Islamic for many of the "conservative" or "Holy Alliance" members in Ozal's Motherland Party, they simply transferred their support to the Prosperity Party.[106] Islamic leaning votes and politicians whose support and power became visible during the October 1991 elections, were therefore previously not as visible under the banner and leadership of Ozal's Western valued vision. When these politicians and their votes abandoned Ozal for the true Islamic activist party, the Prosperity Party, they became immediately visible. This new visibility of Islamic votes and politicians, which had

---

[105]Ahmad, 19.

[106]These are two terms used by fellow ANAP members in describing the Islamic fudamentalists in their coalition. "Yilmaz Fires Fundamentalists from Key Posts," Nokta, FBIS, 28 Jul 91.

existed all along under the Motherland Party, was then incorrectly construed by some scholars and the media as an increase in Islamic power at the polls.

In fact, the 1 November 1991 "success" of the Prosperity Party is really neither novel, nor much of a victory at all when compared with the electoral standings of the National Salvation Party (the precursor to the Prosperity Party) in the 1970's.[107] In the analysis to follow concerning percentages of votes and assembly seats, two aspects of the Turkish electoral system should be kept in mind. First, "Since 1950, elections have been based on fully direct suffrage..." Therefore straight comparisons of percentages of votes for the various elections can be made without distorting a party's strength. Second, from 1969-1980, the "Simple d'Hondt System" a proportional system for representation, was used to determine the number of seats alloted to each party in parliament, provided they met a minimum requirement of ten percent of the national vote. This system provides a "bonus of seats" to the party which wins the plurality of the votes. Consequently, a comparison of percentage of votes won by the various parties to be discussed is a more accurate representation of party

---

[107]George E. Delury, ed., World Encyclopedia of Political Systems and Parties, 2nd ed., Vol. 2. (new York: Facts on File Publications, 1987), 1122-1123.

strength than is a comparison of the number of parliament seats each party holds.

In 1974, Necmettin Erbakan, then leader of the National Salvation Party, was Deputy Prime Minister in a coalition government with the winner of the 14 Oct 1973 elections, the Republican People's Party (Cumhuriyet Halk Partisi).[108] Erbakan had been invited to form a coalition with the Republican People's Party after winning 11.8 percent of the vote, and placing fourth in the polls. More importantly, they had 48 seats in the assembly, the third largest block. See Table 3, Appendix B on page 117, for the 1973 election results.[109] In this coalition government, the National Salvation Party was allotted seven of the 24 cabinet posts for their politicians. The remainder belonged to the dominant Republican People's Party.[110]

In 1975, in another coalition government, the National Salvation Party held eight of the 30 cabinet posts. This was the second largest block of cabinet posts in this coalition government.[111]

---

[108]Geoffrey Lewis, Modern Turkey (New York: Praeger Publishers, 1974), 197.

[109]Ibid., 196.

[110]Ibid., 197.

[111]Ibid.

By comparison, the Prosperity Party in the November 1991 elections was not invited by Sulyeman Demirel's True Path Party, the winner of the elections, to join in the coalition government. This completely shut them out of the cabinet and official government access. Furthermore, while they received 16.88 percent of the popular votes in this election, apparently five percent more than in 1973, they were still only fourth in the polls.

The Prosperity Party was also not alone in capturing this 16.88 percent of the vote and 52 parliament seats. In fact, the Prosperity Party ran in the election as a coalition partner with two other right-wing parties, the Nationalist Labor Party (Milliyetci Calisma Partisi), and the Reformist Democratic Party (Islahatci Demokrasi Partisi).[112] These two parties ran as candidates under the banner of the Welfare Party when they anticipated they would not meet the barrier of obtaining the necessary ten percent of the vote for legislative representation.[113]

The Nationalist Work Party is considered to be the successor of another of the outlawed parties following the 12 Sept 1980 coup, the extreme right-wing Nationalist Action

---

[112]Arthur S. Banks, ed., Political Handbook of the World: 1992 (Binghamton, New York: CSA Publications, 1992), 783.

[113]Ibid.

50

Party (Milliyetci Harekat Partisi).[114] If this extreme
right-wing, but not Islamic fundamentalist, Nationalist
Action Party's election results for the lower house of the
assembly are reviewed from the 1960's until 1977,[115] it
shows this party had various levels of support as high as 14
percent in 1961, to as low as 2.2 percent of the vote in
1965. See Table 4, Appendix C on page 118. Averaging
their support for the lower house elections in 1969, 1973
and 1977, their level of support was 4.26 percent for that
period.[116]

Thus, it would be a conservative estimate to assume that
the Nationalist Labor Party element of the Prosperity Party
coalition received roughly between 2.2 percent (its lowest
support in 1965), to 4.26 percent of the vote (its average
between 1969 and 1977) in the 1991 elections. If this
support for the Nationalist Labor Party is subtracted from
the 16.88 percent of the vote which went to the coalition
with the Prosperity Party in 1991, then the Prosperity Party
only realized a scant increase of 0.82 to 2.88 percent over

---

[114]Ibid.

[115]Under the old 1961 Turkish Constitution, there was a
bicameral legislature comprised of a lower house and a senate.
Under the 1982 Constitution a unicameral body was established.
Pitman, 393.

[116]George S. Harris, Turkey: Coping with Crisis (Boulder,
Colorado: Westview Press, 1985), 137.

its 1973 election results, when it received its highest percentage of votes for the lower house of parliament.[117]

Sabri Sayari, noted scholar on Turkey, who is presently at the National Academy of Science, has also expressed similar doubts as to the increase of fundamentalist strength at the polls, as represented in votes for the Prosperity Party. He also suggests that when the votes for the nationalists are separated from those of the fundamentalists in the former Prosperity Party coalition, that the fundamentalists have only realized perhaps a one percent increase in popularity over the last two decades.[118] This hardly constitutes evidence for claiming a serious threat of Islamic fundamentalism through the electoral process.

This conclusion is further supported by events between this coalition after their entry into parliament. At that time, 19 of the 52 members of the Grand National Assembly

---

[117]These calculations are based on a comparison between the figures from election results for seats in the present Grand National Assembly and the lower house of the assembly prior to the 1980 coup. Election results for the Senate, prior to its elimination under the 1982 Constitution, are discounted since the former lower house of the assembly comes closest to approximating the new Grand National Assembly. Nevertheless, if the lowest percentage of votes for the National Action Party in the senate were taken, 1.9 percent in 1966, and the average of their percentage from 1968-1977 were used, 3.63 percent, similar figures would result.

[118]Dr. Sabri Sayari, National Academy of Science, Telephone conversation with author, 23 Mar 93.

elected under the Prosperity Party's name reverted back to the Nationalist Labor Party. Three other members of this coalition reentered the Reformist Democratic Party. In reality, only 30 Prosperity Party members were elected to the Grand National Assembly, not 52.[119] A full 42.3 percent of the votes which went to the Prosperity Party actually represented support for the ultra-nationalist candidates, not necessarily fundamentalist, members of the coalition. Subtracting the support for the nationalists elements of this coalition from the reported 16.88 percent of the votes which went to the Prosperity Party, it becomes clear that Erbakan's group actually only received 9.74 percent of the vote for the Grand National Assembly. This figure is actually less than the percentage they received in 1973. Overall then, the true percentage of votes which went to the fundamentalist Prosperity Party in October 19ɔ_, is no better than in 1973, when they had their best showing. It would be fair to say then that these figures more accurately reflect a hollow victory and stagnation on the part of the fundamentalists, not some sort of spectacular "volcano" of growing nation-wide support for a politically resurgent Islam in Turkey.

---

[119]Figures related to events after the election come from Banks, 783.

The Prosperity Party's November 1991 election results
are still less impressive considering the indirect
assistance Islam has received in recent years from the
powerful Turkish military. The military has long recognized
that the real internal threat to Turkey over the last twenty
years has been the radical left, not the Islamic activists.
It is the left which has the best organized, largest and
most violent terrorist groups. Of the roughly 80 terrorist
groups known to exist in Turkey, only 16 are oriented
towards radical Islam.[120] The majority are leftists.

Of these leftist threats, the supreme challenge to
Turkey's stability at this time is the well known Kurdish
threat, embodied in the Kurdish Workers' Party (PKK). As the
name implies, this group espouses a mixture of
Marxist-Leninist ideology and Kurdish nationalism.[121] Since
1984, when PKK attacks began in earnest, this group has
claimed the lives of approximately 5,000 people. Other
groups, such as the violent Revolutionary Left (Dev Sol)
also follow a Marxist-Leninist ideology and have targeted
key officers of the military and security forces, among
others, for assassination. In just one year, between

[120]"Active Terrorist Groups in Country Detailed," Cumhuriyet,
FBIS, 20 Oct 91.

[121]Michael M. Gunter, "The Kurdish Problem in Turkey,' Middle
East Journal, Vol. 42, No. 3 (Summer, 1988), 395.

1990-1991, Dev Sol assassinated 45 people, some of whom were prominent generals in the 1980 military coup. The radical Islamic groups have been far more restrained in their actions, killing far fewer people than the left since the military returned stability to the state in the early 1980's.[122]

To combat the real problem of the radical left, the military attempted to use Islam as a weapon against leftist ideology. This military support of Islam was translated into permission to teach more religion in schools and tolerance of the expansion and influence of sufi orders in Quranic schools and students' hostels.[123] Groups such as the Prosperity Party thus indirectly benefited by the military's attitude towards Islam during the 1980's. It is surprising then that the Islamic front of Erbakan's Prosperity Party still trails the leftists in votes and that they did not realize an increase in votes over their 1973 showing.

Lastly, in regard to the Prosperity Party's alleged victory in November 1991, the question must be asked what the rational was for the 16.88 percent of voters who

---

[122]I am not callous to this loss of life, but am simply comparing the almost minuscule efforts of the Islamic terrorists when compared to leftist groups in Turkey.

[123]Ahmad, 18.

supported this coalition. This answer can be partially derived by examining which segments of the population support this party. As detailed information is not available about voter support for the Prosperity Party, information can be extrapolated from work conducted on electoral results in relation to the National Salvation Party. This is reasonable considering the party leadership and the platforms of the Prosperity and National Salvation Parties are similar.

A 1973 survey of votes for the Prosperity Party's predecessor, the National Salvation Party, disclosed 67.2 percent of all their votes were from rural areas, whereas the remaining 32.8 percent of its votes came from urban sectors.[124] As Binnaz Toprak of Bogazici University in Istanbul said,

> In an overwhelming majority of the 67 administrative districts in Turkey, the NSP polled most of its votes from the countryside. Only in five administrative districts- Istanbul, Ankara, Izmir, Adana, and Eskisehir- did the NSP fare better in urban centers.[125]

These figures do not lend themselves to an apparent pattern of support. However, independent work on the significance of this data, conducted by Toprak, and on the

---

[124]Binnaz Toprak, Islam and Political Development in Turkey (Leiden, the Netherlands: E.J.Brill, 1981), 110.

[125]Ibid.

functions of religion in Turkish society, by Ahmet Yucekok, reveals some very critical thinking which sheds a great deal of light as to the groups and reasons which sustain the Islamicists in Turkey.

First, Toprak believes the Islamicists, as represented by the National Salvation Party, and later the Prosperity Party, attract the support of "marginal" elements within Turkish society.[126] These elements, "on the margins of modern industrial society," are groups not closely integrated into the mainstream because of either social or economic reasons.[127] Thus, the 32.8 percent of the NSP's votes in 1973, which were obtained in urban areas, come from economically marginal elements. Toprak wrote the following about this matter:

> Istanbul, Ankara, Izmir, and Adana score highest in the development index that the State Planning Organization (Devlet Planlama Teskilati) has put out. Eskisehir occupies the eighth place and has had a high rate of industrialization in recent years. Being the most developed industrial centers, they contain large numbers of people who have been adversely affected by industrialization, such as small traders and artisans. In Istanbul, for example, the NSP received the highest percentage of its votes from Beykoz, Eminozu, Eyup and Fatih in the 1973 election. Three out of four of these electoral districts- Eminonu, Eyup and Fatih- differ from others in the city in their cultural and economic traditionalism. Eminonu is a business district but it is more a business center of small

---

[126]Ibid., 104-105.

[127]Ibid., 105.

traders and artisans (the famous Grand Bazaar is located here) than big industries.[128]

In short, areas within the urban population centers of Turkey where the traditional economic patterns of the small artisan, trader, and shopkeeper have been disrupted by rapid industrialization are likely to support the Islamicists.

In the rural areas supportive of the Islamicists, Toprak believes this can be explained by the, "cultural traditionalism of the Turkish countryside."[129] The appeal of the rural segments of society to Erbakan's platform, particularly its religious tones, makes sense when considering that, "religion probably functions to reinforce traditional social or economic relationships," in these less developed areas.[130] The following is what Toprak had to say about the influence of traditionalism in the countryside:

> If we can assume that the NSP's appeal to voters in general is mainly religious, then we can also assume that the party will have a stronger base in rural areas than in urban since rural Turkey is markedly more traditional than the urban. As I have pointed out in earlier chapters, Turkish peasants have been much slower than urban residents in accepting the idea of a secular state, especially one which controls religious activity. Peasant communities are tradition-bound, and for Turkish peasants, much of tradition stems from

---

[128]Ibid., 110.

[129]Ibid., 112.

[130]Ibid., 117.

Islam. Hence, they would be more amenable to vote for a party, such as the NSP, which has established a religious image for itself and which promises, at least implicitly, to guide Turkish society along Islamic principles.[131]

This would seem to imply that rural votes for the NSP are genuinely religious in nature. However, Toprak goes on to say later that this is not clearly established. He writes:

> Eastern Anatolia [a rural area of Turkey] is a region where landlords (aga) and religious sheikhs are very powerful in local communities and where their political preferences are often reflected among the voters during elections. In the case of the NSP, it is reasonable to assume that much of its support in Eastern Anatolia can be connected to "dependency voting," namely, voting on the basis of not individual choice but rather, on the basis of pressure from a local patron, a religious leader, or the like.[132]

In rural areas then, the stronghold of the Islamicists' votes in Turkey during the 1970's, Islam is an appealing platform. But in this sense, Islam is a tool to reinforce traditional patterns. Are the voters in rural areas, or for that matter the peasants who move into the shantytowns of the large cities and still maintain many traditional values, then actually voting to establish some theocratic regime for the sake of Islam, or are they simply expressing a more basic desire to maintain society as they know it?

---

[131]Ibid., 112-113.

[132]Ibid., 117.

Furthermore, one can only wonder what the true strength of
the NSP's support in rural areas would have been in the
absence of "dependency voting."

Second, Ahmet Yucekok conducted a study of religious
organizations in Turkey (Yucekok, 1971), which has led to
findings that Islam in Turkey has a dual purpose.[133] "In
the less developed areas, religious ties reinforce dominant
power relationships. In the more developed areas, it becomes
a means of protest for individuals who have lost their
economic base as a result of rapid change."[134]

Hence, when combining the work of Toprak and Yucekok,
the notion that supporters, in this case voters, for Islamic
parties in Turkey are themselves Islamic fundamentalists
becomes rather tenuous. This led Toprak to conclude the
following:

> If we combine the two observations [his view and
> Yucekok's], the picture that emerges suggests that the
> NSP appealed either to rural people who have remained
> in their traditional communities or to individuals who
> have a marginal status in terms of their cultural
> orientation and economic status. **In rural
> underdeveloped areas, the NSP vote probably indicated
> support for tradition**...Although the religious issue
> cannot be considered the most important determinant of
> electoral success, it nevertheless played an important

---

[133]Binnaz Toprak, "Politicisation of Islam in a Secular State:
The National Salvation Party in Turkey," in From Nationalism to
Revolutionary Islam, ed. Said Amir Arjomand (Albany, New York:
State University of New York Press, 1984), 131.

[134]Ibid.

role in mobilization of the countryside...**On the Other hand, the fact that the *NSP's* support also came from rapidly changing communities may indicate a protest vote by individuals who have been unable to make the transition to new kinds of economic activity.** For example, it is probably not by chance that the electoral districts of Istanbul where the NSP received the highest percentage of its votes are centres of small merchants, artisans, and shopkeepers.[135]

While these conclusions are derived primarily from work in the 1970's, there does not appear to be any reason to negate these findings. It is still true that the "new town-dwellers," a euphemism for those living in the squatter villages (gecekondus) which surround the major cities of Western Turkey, are suggested to be the segment of Turkish society most attracted to Erbakan's Prosperity party.[136]

The immediate assumption in Turkey and other areas of the Muslim World where Islamic parties are challenging the government, is that voters for these parties are themselves Islamic activists. It should now be clear from the proceeding discussion that those supporting the Islamicists in Turkey, as well as in other countries, do so for a variety of reasons not always connected with Islamic fanaticism. To address this problem at a more general level, it is worth turning to the insight of Professor Metin Heper

---

[135]Emphasis added. Ibid., 132-133.

[136]"Islam Returns to Politics," The Economist, February 27th-March 5th 1993, 58.

of Bogazici University in Istanbul on these matters. He stated the following:

> Nor is the Islam of the ruled a homogenous entity. In one relatively secularized country, Turkey, I found that for some (i.e., transitionals), Islam emerged in the garb of a Durkheimian version of religiosity, whereas for others (the educated elite), it had a metaphysical function. Thus, it offered a psychological solution for one group, a cultural one for the other. Even more telling is the classification made by Bill and Leiden of adherents of the Muslim Brotherhood in Egypt, a surprising number of whom are young and middle-class. There are those who have been attracted by expediency, those who have assuaged nostalgic guilt by supporting a religious posture that they have found increasingly uncomfortable, those who are genuinely bewildered (i.e., who wonder whether the secular age they have entered is truly right and who have often become alienated from a system that they see as corrupt, unjust and venal) and, finally, those who are outright fanatics.[137]

It is almost certain that in Turkey, as with the Muslim Brotherhood in Egypt, many of those voting or supporting Erbakan's Prosperity Party were attracted to his message for various reasons. Some of these reasons might include traditionalism, justice, morality, improved economic prosperity, out of frustration with corruption, or simply to spite the ruling parties. These concepts are not a monopoly held solely by the Islamicists. It is symbolic in this sense that the Prosperity Party's flag is a golden staff of wheat,

---

[137]Metin Heper, "Islam, Politics and Change in the Middle East," in Islam and Politics in the Modern Middle East, ed. Metin Heper and Raphael Israeli (New York: St Martin's Press, 1984), 5.

an obvious symbol of "prosperity," not necessarily Islam, on the red background of Turkey's present flag.

C. LIMITATIONS ON THE GROWTH OF PROSPERITY PARTY STRENGTH

Clearly, from the preceding analysis it is obvious that the present electoral threat of Islamic fundamentalism to Turkey is more cosmetic than real. The Prosperity Party is no closer to gaining control of the state apparatus than it was in the 1970's, when complaints were few about it being "fundamentalist." Yet, in spite of the above analysis demonstrating the present lukewarm response by the majority of Turkish voters to Erbakan's platform, questions will persist about the future prospects and ability of this party to challenge the secularism of the state. Namely, is it possible that the Prosperity Party could eventually come to power? And, if so, what could be expected by such a government?

As already established, the likelihood of Erbakan's Prosperity Party becoming a major force among Turkish political groups in the near future is very unlikely as reflected in its recent and historical polling. More importantly though, the very basic nature of Erbakan's message will clash with elements of Turkish society. This will limit this party from ever gathering sufficient electoral strength to become anything more than a junior

63

partner in a coalition government, rather than a mass-based entity with widespread popular appeal able to capture the reins of the state for itself.

One of these elements of Turkish society which will militate the power of Erbakan's Islamicists in the electoral process are the Alevis of Turkey. According to the Turkish use of this word, Alevi is synonymous to Shia Islam.[138] However, the Alevis of Turkey are themselves split along ethnic and sectarian lines. For instance, the Alevis include the main sect of Shia Islam, the "Twelver Shia," as well as the "Alevi proper," who are considered by the Twelver Shia as heretics.[139] Although not much is known of their practices because of this sect's secretive nature, what is known of the Alevis differs greatly from the Twelver Shia and Sunni in religious practices and beliefs. Their very name, Alevi, or "Alawites" as they are known in Syria, exemplifies these differences. As Paul Pitman succinctly wrote:

> Whereas the Sunni profession of faith attests to the oneness of God and asserts that "Muhammad is his Prophet," Twelver Shia adds the phrase "and Ali is the Friend (or Saint) of God." The Alevis go even further by believing in some form of incarnation of God in Ali

---

[138]Pitman, 125.

[139]Ibid., 126. From this point on I will use the term "Alevi" to refer to those who believe in the divinity of Ali, not the Twelver Shia.

and recite a formula of faith that indicates that "Ali is my God" (whence their designation Ali-Ilahis).[140]

It is further suggested that the Alevi have absorbed some practices and beliefs from other religions including Zoroastrianism, Christianity, Judaism and gnosticism.[141] Evidence to this point includes their observance of both Christmas and Easter, which would be anathema to either the dominant Sunni of Turkey, or the Twelver Shia.[142]

The Alevis are further divided among ethnic Arab, Kurdish and Turkish believers. This, as Pitman has rightly pointed out, creates segments of Turkey's society which are separated from the mainstream Turkish-Sunni element by ethnic or religious lines, or in some cases both.[143]

As a result of these religious and ethnic differences, the Alevi have for centuries been the subject of much distrust and violence by the Turkish-Sunni majority. Furthermore, the historical legacy of the Ottomans and the early Republic, which used these ethnic and sectarian differences as a means of maintaining power and forging a

---

[140]Ibid.

[141]Ibid.

[142]Professor Kamil T. Said, Naval Postgraduate School, NS 4300, Islamic Civilization, Syllabus, July 1984, 46.

[143]Pitman, 126.

national identity, continues to persist. Taner Timur,

formerly of Ankara University wrote:

> In the nineteenth century, Ottoman statesman took
> advantage of the tensions and conflicts among the
> nationalities in order to stay in power; since
> republican Turkey is based upon the foundation of a
> homogenous nation-with the exception of the Kurdish
> people-those conflicts were replaced by struggles
> between leftist and rightist extremism, occasionally
> cloaked under religious guise such as strife
> between Alevis (shi'ites) and Sunnis.[144]

This hatred and violence leveled at this secretive sect

of Islam is not a phenomenon of the distant past.

During the 1970's, much of the violence indigenous to Turkey

between extreme left and right-wing groups was again

translated into Sunni attacks on the Alevi, this time at the

instigation of ultra-nationalists, for reasons of political

expediency. The low point of this Alevi-Sunni violence

was the Sunni attack on a group of Shia Muslims in

Kahramanmaras in 1978, in which over one hundred people,

mostly Shias, were killed during a funeral procession.[145]

Part of the reason for this violence against the Alevi

as recently as the 1970's, was their mislabeling as

---

[144]Taner Timur, "The Ottoman Heritage," in Turkey in Transition, ed. Irvin C. Schick and Ertugrul Ahmet Tonak (Oxford: Oxford University Press, 1987), 20.

[145]Howard A. Reed, "Ataturk's Secularizing Legacy and the Continuing Vitality of Islam in Republican Turkey," in Islam in the Contemporary World, ed. Cyriac K. Pullapilly (Notre Dame, Indiana: Cross Roads Books, 1980), 336-337.

leftists, by extreme right-wing nationalists. The Alevis were actually not leftists, but have traditionally supported political parties which, through adherence to secularist values, would best serve to protect their rights as a much maligned minority group. A key example of this support of the secular left is demonstrated by events in the 1973 elections, when tremendous Alevi support was registered for the Republican People's Party (Cumhuriyet Halk Partisi), Ataturk's own party. In this election, the slogan of this party was, "left of center."[146] As Professor Caglar Keyder wrote, the Alevis of Turkey overwhelmingly supported the Republican People's Party because, "They had confidence in the traditional commitment of the RPP to secularism and its willingness to uphold the rights of a religious minority."[147] The Alevis were at that time estimated at between five and 12 million people, out of Turkey's overall population of 41 million people, as listed in 1977.[148]

This adherence of the Alevi community to political groups espousing secularist values is still intact. As Turkish reporter Miyase Ilknur recently commented during

[146]Caglar Keyder, "The Political Economy of Turkish Democracy," in Turkey in Transition, 55.

[147]Ibid., 56.

[148]Ibid.

the December 1991, negotiations to place Alevis in the important Department of Religious Affairs, "to some they are a block of votes that must be won, to others, insurance for the secular state as opposed to sharia, and to others, representatives of progressive, modern thought."[149] Notably, these discussions, which involved the then newly elected Prime Minister Demirel, as well as other meetings between key politicians and the Alevi, were held in a semi-secretive manner. While the importance of the Alevi vote can not be ignored, it is still believed to be politically risky to openly court their support. As Ilknur continued to say, "any politician who announces in public that he will grant the rights the Alawis want runs the risk of drawing upon himself the displeasure of the religious sector with its prior conditioning."[150] With the continued inequality of the Alevis within Turkish society, it can be deduced from this statement that they are neither likely to change their traditional secularist voting patterns in the near future, nor will Erbakan risk alienating his base of power by courting Alevi favor to increase his votes.

_____

[149]"Efforts to Unite Religious Groups Discussed," NOKTA, FBIS, 15 Dec 19.

[150]Ibid.

Today, the Alevis are thought to comprise as much as 20 percent of Turkey's total population of 58 million.[151] This is not an unsubstantial number. As Erbakan's platform is based on Sunni Islam, and at times sounds very uncharitable to anyone not Muslim, presumably Sunni Muslim, there seems little logic to support the belief that this substantial minority will abandon its traditional voting pattern of supporting the more open minded and secularist political parties of the left. A full 20 percent of Turkey's population is therefore completely lost as votes for Erbakan in future elections before the campaigning even begins.

Another considerable barrier for Erbakan's party to overcome before it could achieve real electoral success is the strength of the block of left-of-center voters. In the October 1991 elections, the two primary left-of-center parties, the Democratic Left Party (Demokratik Sol Parti, DSP) and the Social Democratic Populist Party (Soysal Demokrat Halkci Parti, SHP), gathered a combined 31.50 percent of the vote (Refer to Table 1). This vote for these two left-of-center parties is roughly 15 percent more than the Islamic activists are officially listed as receiving in 1991 (16.88 percent). The gap between the votes

[151]Alasdair Drysdale and Gerald H. Blake, The Middle East and North Africa: A Political Geography (Oxford: Oxford University Press, 1985), 178.

for the left and the Islamicists grows even wider in favor of the left, when applying earlier analysis. This disclosed the Prosperity Party received closer to ten percent, not 16.88 percent, of the vote. In reality then, the two major political organizations which openly refer to themselves as parties of the left, received approximately three times as many votes than the fundamentalists. Yet, in the new political landscape which espouses the green "threat" of Islam over the fading red menace of communism, no one is rushing to warn of the dangers of the left in Turkey. It would be interesting to review the literature of the 1970's, when the Cold War and the fear of the left dominated political thinking in the West, and "fundamentalism" was not yet the household word and concern of today, to see if there was anxiety in the West over the rise of the National Salvation Party.

The prognosis for future voters shifting from this pattern of supporting the left also does not in favor the Islamicists. In a poll conducted in September 1991, just weeks prior to the elections, 19 and 20 year-olds living in the three major cities of Ankara, Istanbul, and Izmir, who were voting for the first time, were asked which party they preferred.[152] See Table 5, Appendix D, on page 119 for the results. What these preferrences indicate is that for male voters, fully 42 percent supported parties of the left. For female voters, the results were even more impressive with 47.9 percent supporting the left. When compared to the percentage of people who actually voted for the two major parties of the left in the October 1991 elections, which resulted in a combined 31.50 percent, the apparent trend among younger voters (as represented by this poll) is towards the left, not the right. This seemingly youthful inclination towards the more secularists and liberal left-of-center parties represents another barrier to the ability of Erbakan to increase the strength of his party as measured in Turkey's electoral process.

D. THE PROSPERITY PARTY IN A COALITION GOVERNMENT

Despite the apparent weaknesses in the ability of the Prosperity Party to compete for support of what analysis indicates to be rather large segments of the Turkish population, and regardless of its stagnant performance in the 1991 Grand National Assembly elections, the possibility

---

[152]It is not known how well this poll adhered to accepted reseach methods and cannot therefore be concluded to be conclusive proof of voting patters. This is also not to say though that this poll was not accurate. It was conducted by "Zet-Medya," which may be a credible polling agency. "Poll on Voting Preferences Among Youth," Tempo, 8-14 Sept 91.

exists that Erbakan could always be invited to form a future coalition government. The fragmented nature of the Turkish electorate, in which a single party often does not win a decisive amount of votes to form a government, creates the possibility that the Islamicists may be touted as a necessary measure of achieving majority rule in the parliament by one of the more dominant parties. This is particularly true when the major mainstream Turkish parties refuse to cooperate with each other in a coalition. This scenario, as alluded to earlier in this paper, occurred on three separate occasions during the 1970's,[153] in which Erbakan was even appointed Deputy Prime Minister. Therefore, if the Prosperity Party could come to have direct influence in the government by riding in on the coat-tails of a larger party, what is to prevent them from enacting Islamic fundamentalist reforms? The answer is nothing, if they have their coalition partner's support.

However, this answer should not produce consternation that Turkey will be taken down a "Muslim Path" if the Prosperity Party becomes fortunate enough to be invited to

---

[153]NSP based coalitions included the Republican People's Party-NSP 1973-1974 coalition, and, "Suleyman Demirel's first and second National Front governments of 1975-77 and 1977-78, respectively." Binnaz Toprak, "Politicisation of Islam in a Secular State: The National Salvation Party in Turkey," in From Nationalism to Revolutionary Islam, 129.

form a future coalition government. Even when Erbakan and
his deputies held important portfolios in the various
governments of the 1970's, their inclination was more
towards industrialization, not Islam. A short review of the
Republican People's Party (RPP)-National Salvation Party
coalition which lasted from January-July 1974 is
particularly insightful in establishing this fact.

On 13 January 1974, Erbakan accepted the invitation of
Bulent Ecevit, the leader of the RPP, to form a coalition
government.[154] The two leaders then began work on a, "joint
protocol" which "virtually became the government's
programme."[155] The protocol for this coalition contained 23
principle clauses, which might be reflective of what the
Islamicists would possibly attempt to accomplish today if in
power. The 23 principal elements of this joint programme,
which both parties agreed to and made public, included the
following:

(1) implement a general amnesty which would include those
convicted of crimes of thought and forest offenses, as
well as former Democrats who had been deprived of civil
rights, to whom they would be restored;
(2) reduce the voting age to 18 years, except for high
school students;
(3) make public servants liable to prosecution not only
for abuse of office, but also for dereliction of duty;

---

[154]Feroz Ahmad, The Turkish Experiment in Democracy 1950-1975
(Boulder, Colorado: Westview Press, 1977), 336.

[155]Ibid.

(4) establish a more equitable system of taxation;

(5) prevent waste in bureaucracy;

(6) legalize the ownership of gecekondus-homes built without permission by rural migrants-constructed up to the end of 1973;

(7) accelerate technical education in secondary schools, and to abolish university entrance examinations;

(8) support the co-operative movement in rural areas and to found a co-operatives bank which would be supervised by the Ministry of Rural Affairs and Co-operatives;

(9) employ foreign exchange reserves for the development of the country in the best possible way; and to encourage co-operatives and 'people's enterprises' to use bank credits;

(10) take measures to provide agricultural credits to the peasant to free him from the need to resort to middlemen and usurers;

(11) establish a minimum price for agricultural produce, and to announce it as early as possible in order to safeguard the producer from having to sell at very low prices;

(12) ensure the efficiency of co-operatives in the marketing of agricultural produce, and to prevent artificial price increases;

(13) find a solution to, and end, the unjust treatment of the opium poppy growers;

(14) change the name of the Ministry of Agriculture to the Ministry of Food-Agriculture and Animal Husbandry [to reflect new and wider functions];

(15) make the operation of public [state] enterprises more democratic, permitting employees to participate in their administration, and to share the profits;

(16) formulate an industrial policy for the expansion of heavy industry-especially capital goods-and to set up a national armaments industry;

(17) promote regionally balanced industrialization, in keeping with a geographical balance and social justice;

(18) limit to a reasonable amount the transfer abroad of profits by foreign investors;

(19) rely on water and coal to produce electrical energy;

(20) place under state control the exploitation of underground mineral resources, including borax; to re-examine the Petroleum Law and amend those clauses which contravene national interests;

(21) import through public companies or co-operatives those goods whose price increases very sharply as a result of shortages;

(22) introduce unemployment insurance, and give priority

74

to old people without means, and cripples;
(23) remain within the joint security system and the existing alliances, but at the same time to increase Turkey's ability to defend herself, and to place under state control joint Turkish-American bases and establishments.[156]

Notice, not one of these guidelines for the administration of this government included anything which could be even remotely interpreted as an act of "Islamic fundamentalism." The emphasis of this program was obviously industrialization. This, however, does not mean the National Salvation Party abandoned its party stance for the chance to be part of the ruling coalition. On the contrary, Erbakan originally declined an offer by Ecevit to form a government three months before he finally agreed in January 1974. Instead, what must be recognized is that, as scholar Binnaz Toprak and others have noted, "the problem of industrialization occupied the most important dimension of party ideology."[157] From this point, Erbakan's occasional unintelligible rambling about industrialization and Islam, and Islam's role in this relationship, can begin to be understood. As Toprak wrote,

---

[156]While lengthy, the entire 23 points are included so the reader could determine for himself the conspicuous absence of "Islamic' goals. Ibid, 336-337.

[157]Binnaz Toprak, "Politicisation of Islam in a Secular State." 125-126.

Turkey had lost its leading position as a great power
because it had failed to industrialize. The NSP
promised to initiate rapid development through
revitalizing indigenous cultural values which would
supply the necessary spiritual and moral qualities for a
new work ethic.[158]

Therefore, Islam's role, as the National Salvation Party espoused it, appears more as a catalyst for industrialization than as an end in itself. The final result of this interaction between industrialization and Islam is a reinvigorated Turkey, worthy of the state's historical legacy. This actually makes a great deal of sense. If, as Erbakan might argue, Turkey (actually the Ottoman Empire) was once the most powerful empire of its era, and Islam was present in both its glory years and later downfall, Islam can not be blamed for its decline. Islam was a positive force for the Ottomans which fueled a gazi (warrior) instinct- leading to greatness. Instead, it was the lack of industrialization which led the Ottomans from the pinnacle of Suleyman's success to the offensive sobriquet of the "sick man of Europe." Islam is therefore not to be dispensed with, but remolded as a Muslim version of the Protestant work ethic in order to obtain industrialization. This led Toprak and fellow scholar Ilkay Sunar to conclude that Islam for the NSP had become "an instrument of

---

[158]Ibid., 126.

76

modernization...something more to be 'believed' than to be 'lived.'"[159] Quoting Clifford Geertz, they further recognized, "the 'tense intermixture', of puritanism and 'determined modernism', and the 'steeping backward in order better to leap' into cultural change and modernity."[160]

These conclusions, which place Islam in a supporting role subservient to industrialization, are evident in the symbolic, but never threatening actions taken by Erbakan in the name of Islam while Deputy Prime Minister. Notable among these harmless gestures was the removal of a sculpture of a nude female from Istanbul Square, officially entitled "Beautiful Istanbul," which had been erected to commemorate the 50th anniversary of the Republic.[161] The NSP referred to this art as "the sculpture of shame," and had it removed by the authority of the Minister of the Interior who was an NSP member. Its removal was predicated on the believe of NSP members that it constituted pornographic material.[162] Other token gestures included the taking of legal action against

---

[159]Ilkay Sunar and Binnaz Toprak, "Islam in Politics: The Case of Turkey," Government and Opposition, Vol. 18, No. 4. (Autumn, 1983), 438-439.

[160]Clifford Geertz, Islam Observed, (Chicago: The University of Chicago Press, 1968) in "Islam in Politics," 439.

[161]Ahmad, The Turkish Experiment in Democracy 1950-1975, 340.

[162]Toprak, "Politicisation of Islam in a Secular State," 124.

the state-owned television station for presenting a documentary on Amazon tribes which included some nudity, and the rejection of a request for government credit to build a tourist resort on the grounds that "tourists corrupt the morality of the Turkish people."[163]

Albeit controversial, and contentious enough to generate sensationalistic headlines, these events hardly represent a serious attempt to undermine secularism and supplant it with Islamic fundamentalism. In fact, Feroz Ahmad interprets these events as simple acts of political expediency. As he suggested, the leadership of the National Salvation Party was concerned that as a junior coalition partner to the Republican People's Party in 1974, their party was losing its distinctiveness. Concerns grew that, because the coalition was working so smoothly, if the NSP did not attempt to reestablish its own identity in the public's eye, then the party would be assured of losing some of its constituents in future elections to the RPP and other parties of the right. A campaign of sorts was therefore established by the NSP to display its independence from the dominant RPP through issues which, "would assure controversy in the press, irritate the intelligentsia, and appeal to the

---

[163]Ibid., 124-125.

traditional values of the petty bourgeoisie."[164] Importantly though, actions were taken which would not endanger the coalition.[165] It was actually Bulent Ecevit, head of the RPP, who would later dissolve the coalition and call for new elections, believing his party had garnered enough support to win a majority for itself.[166]

Summing up this section then, it can be said that Islam for the most important Islamic party in Turkey, is subservient to industrialization. Furthermore, when changes were enacted by the Islamicists in the government, these constituted token expressions, never anything truly serious which would threaten the state. All of this was apparently understood by the voters. A joke heard during the 1973 election campaign is particularly revealing about this point. The joke asked, "Why is the National Salvation Party like a water-melon? Because it's green (the Prophet's color) outside and red inside. What Erbakan was preaching was indeed a kind of Islamic socialism."[167] If actions do count for more than empty political speeches, the lesson is that his calls for increased Islamic values in the state should

---

[164]Ahmad, The Turkish Experiment in Democracy 1950-1975, 340.

[165]Ibid.

[166]Ibid., 341.

[167]Lewis, 195-196.

79

be interpreted as means to an industrialized Turkey, and occasionally as a political ploy for notoriety.

E. THE FINAL SAY OF THE ARMY

The final power which would militate the ability of the Islamicists from ever taking Turkey down the "Muslim path" is the Turkish Armed Forces. It has never been forgotten among military officers that it was General Mustafa Kemal, Ataturk, who led the military to successfully fight off the dismemberment of present day Turkey from the victorious powers of World War I. Ataturk was also the force which instituted reforms which modernized Turkey and brought it into the modern world. To this end, the military has abrogated for itself the responsibility of defending the integrity of Ataturk's principles, which have served as the basis for modern Turkey. This attitude is instilled in every officer of the armed forces. The following is an excerpt of just a small amount of the required reading on Ataturkism at the Turkish military academies:

> The overall task of the Turkish Armed Forces is to protect and guard the Turkish Republic against internal and external threats, and this task should be considered along with Dynamic Ideal of the Turkish State, the Ataturk principles. Ataturk has described the qualities and principles that must always be borne in mind for the strong, harmonious and cooperative functioning of all the institutions within the state, such as Republicanism, Nationalism, Populism, Etatism, Secularism, and the Revolutionary spirit, and demanded that these principles and

qualities be implemented and protected. All these principles and qualities are meant to ensure a strong structure for the Turkish State, which must first be built on sound foundations. The foundation will be strong if it relies on Turkish heroism, Turkish culture, and unites the Turkish nation. The Turkish Armed Forces constitute the unshakable foundation of the state.[168]

Among these principles of Ataturkism, secularism is one of the most heavily emphasized in the training of officers.[169] As former Turkish military officer, now political journalist, Mehmet Ali Birand wrote:

A point underlined in this respect is the possibility that, unless state and religion remain separate, the country may once more revert to a period of decline and may have to surrender to foreign powers as a result of losing touch with developments in the modern world.[170]

On several occasions this training, and the attitude to the protection of secularism it instills, has resulted in direct and indirect military influence on civilian government. Specifically, the armed forces have made a point of only tolerating so much tinkering with secularism before they feel compelled to place Turkey back on the path which Ataturk laid down in the 1920-1930's. On three occasions, in 1960, 1971, and 1980, this military involvement took the form of coups, which took control of the government

---

[168]Mehmet Ali Birand, _Shirts of Steel, An Anatomy of the Turkish Armed Forces_ (London: I.B. Tauris and Co. Ltd, 1991), 84.

[169]Ibid., 63.

[170]Ibid.

for various lengths of time to restore the politics to what they, as the protectors of Ataturkism, felt was the proper path for the Republic.

The event which triggered the 1980 military coup represents one of the more important historical examples that the military will not allow Islamic fundamentalists to divert Turkey from its Ataturkist legacy, let alone create a theocratic state.

On 12 Sept 1980, after several years of ineffective government and increasing violence which left dozens of citizens dead each day, the military staged a coup. However, prior to this coup, the military had issued several warnings to the politicians and had even postponed plans for earlier takeovers of the government. In one warning to the President by General Kenan Evren, Chief of Staff of the Turkish Armed Forces, Evren as well as the top ranking officers of all the services wrote the following:

> It is crystal clear for everyone to see that the main condition for the reestablishment of internal peace and tranquility is to unite all our citizens in an indivisible national spirit under principles which are derived from Ataturkist nationalism. The speediest rescue of the country from its current predicament is amongst the duties not only of governments but of all political parties.[171]

---

[171]Mehmet Ali Birand, The General's Coup in Turkey, An Inside Story of 12 September 1980 (London: Brassey's Defense Publishers, 1987), 100-101.

This statement was merely the cover letter to a declaration by the military entitled simply, "The Views of the Turkish Armed Forces." Included in these views was the following paragraph:

> Our nation has no longer any patience left for those who misuse constitutional freedoms to sing the Communist Internationale instead of our National Anthem, to those who agitate for an Islamic State, for those who yearn for all sorts of fascism, for anarchists, wreckers and secessionists who assault our democratic regime.[172]

Despite this warning, which was issued on 27 Dec 1979, the military had still hoped Turkish politics would right itself without its assistance. It may have been that the military would never have intervened if events had shown some improvement. However, on 6 September 1980, Erbakan organized a mass rally in Konya which, "flouted everything Kemal Ataturk and the Turkish army had ever stood for."[173] During this rally, calls were shouted for the introduction of the Sharia. As analyst Kenneth Mackenzie noted, "Of all the events immediately preceding the coup, the Konya rally has been specially singled out by both

---

[172]Ibid., 102.

[173]Kenneth Mackenzie, <u>Turkey Under the Generals</u>, Publication of the Institute for the Study of Conflict, No. 126 (London: The Institute for the Study of Conflict, 1981), 15.

83

General Evren and General Saltik as a catalytic factor in their decision to intervene."[174]

This attitude towards protecting secularism is one which does not appear to be waning. The Turkish armed forces have gone to great lengths to ensure its officer and conscript ranks remain a force free from politically active Islamic soldiers, as well as extremists of the left. Recent measures have included extensive investigations of all ranks and services and mass dismissals from the services of anyone thought to harbor extremist feelings.[175] With such stringent measures, the Turkish military will remain a force free to counter-balance any extremist attempt to upset the secular cornerstone laid by Ataturk.

F. CONCLUDING REMARKS ON THE ISLAMIC THREAT THROUGH THE ELECTORAL PROCESS

The threat of Islamic fundamentalism to Turkey through its electoral process appears greatly exaggerated. When analyzed, the electoral "victory" of the Welfare Party in the important 20 Oct 1991 elections indicates the Islamicists did not gain much if any support since their 1973 peak. And, among those voting for the Islamicists, one

---

[174]Ibid.

[175]"Rightist Movements in Army, State Detailed," Cumhuriyet, FBIS, 4 Jan 1990, and "Military Discharges Linked to 'Reactionary Views,'" Milliyet, FBIS, 16 Nov 91.

must still question their intentions. Dependency voting, support of tradition, and protest voting are, in my understanding, not clearly equivalent to support for a theocratic state.

It also appears that fairly important segments of the population will militate the ability of the Welfare Party to break its traditional fourth place showing in the polls. As long as the Alevis and other minority groups support parties defending secularism, the block of left-of-center voters remains strong, and the youth favor the left, the Islamicists of Erbakan's party are unlikely to amount to anything but a junior coalition partner.

Finally, and maybe most importantly for those who see the future stability of Turkey threatened by the Islamicists, a strong argument can be made that the Welfare Party is more interested in industrialization, rather than Islamicisation of the state. Nevertheless, the Turkish armed forces have shown in numerous actions that they will not tolerate the disestablishment of Ataturkism and one of its cornerstones - secularism. As this force continues to guard against this phenomenon among its ranks, it is surely gearing itself for the any future contingency.

Based on the above analysis, it can only be concluded that while it may be fashionable to suggest Turkey will, "go

Muslim," there is insufficient evidence to support the claim there is presently a serious Islamic threat to Turkey through its electoral process. And, given that such forces eventually arise, there are powerful forces in Turkish society which will militate against the success of any such movement.

III. EMERGING ISSUES IN SOUTHEAST TURKEY

Up to this point, this thesis has explored recent political and social issues presented by the Western media and certain scholars as evidence of a strong Islamic fundamentalist movement in Turkey. The final issue to be discussed concering Islamic fundamentalism in Turkey, however, is not historical, but just emerging and begining to attract the widespread attention of the Turkish press and elements of Western society.[176] This issue revolves around a new wave of violence unfolding in Turkey's southeast region. Information concerning this violence is still evolving in respect to details and accuracy, and is far from complete. Yet, it is highly probable that those who are drawn into what Philip Robins implied was a fashionable analytical game of guessing which states are likely to "go Muslim," will soon turn to these events in the southeast as proof of the Islamic threat to Turkey. This final section will review the nature of a new rash of violence in the region. This will establish that what appears to be the emergence of an

---

[176]Examples include, "Amnesty: Turkey Lags On Rights" The Washington Post, 11 Nov 1992, A33, and the editorial "In Turkey, Journalists Do Their Job in Peril," by Senators Cohen and Graham and Representatives Green and Lewis, The New York Times, 8 Oct 92, A34.

Islamic fundamentalist terrorist threat is in actuality a conglomeration of Islamic fundamentalist, Kemalist, and religious reactions to the dominant leftist terrorist group in the country, the Kurdish Worker's Party (PKK). And, while substantive information in the open press concerning this movement is weak in some aspects, there are several indicators to suggest that the Islamic fundamentalist terrorist organization involved in this new wave of violence is the least important element.

A. AN OVERVIEW OF THE "ISLAMIC FUNDAMENTALIST" VIOLENCE IN THE TROUBLED SOUTHEAST

The southeast region of Turkey, in which the majority of the people are Kurds, is the traditional area of operation for the extremely violent PKK. The PKK, espousing a mixture of Kurdish nationalism and Marxist-Leninist philosophy, has as its goal the establishment of an independent Kurdistan in what is presently the southeastern and eastern provinces of Turkey. From camps and way stations in the bordering states of Syria, Iraq, and Iran, and from bases in the difficult mountainous terrain within Turkey, the PKK has launched attacks into this region since 1984. These attacks, generally involve hit-and-run operations against small military and Jandarma (rural para-military security forces) posts, police stations, villages, small towns, and even

trains. Often, the numbers of attackers are limited to
approximately 20 people. Occasionally though, the PKK has
launched attacks on more secure targets with as many as 500
militants. In its fight with the state, the PKK has also
resorted to assassinations, bombings, kidnappings, and on
more than one occasion, the complete destruction of Kurdish
villages which oppose their rule. Much of the area is under
martial law. This area is collectively referred to in Turkey
as the "Extraordinary Situation Area." It is not an
exaggeration to say that on any given day there is at least
one article concerning the PKK in the Turkish press.

Recently though, the PKK has had to share their press
exposure with a new and growing wave of violence which also
has its origins in the southeast. This new violence,
nominally at least, involves Islamic fundamentalism.

One aspect of this violence involves what appears to be
a growing radical, grass-roots, Islamic awakening. In 31 Aug
92, the Deputy Director for Religious Affairs, Mehmet Nuri
Yilmaz, advised his department had been forced to withdraw
personnel from six of the ten southeastern provinces under
emergency rule.[177] This directorate of the Turkish Government
is, "an official body within the secular state apparatus in

---

[177]"Official Warns of Religious Extremists in Southeast,"
Anatolia, FBIS, 31 Aug 92.

charge of all 'official' religious affairs."[178] It is responsible for 63,176 personnel working in Turkey's 66,674 mosques.[179] According to Yilmaz, "6,686 authorized religious leaders had faced joint threats from separatist [PKK] and extremist Moslem groups" in the southeast.[180] Furthermore, in March 1993, it was reported in the Turkish Daily News that, "the Ministry of Education sent a team of inspectors to the mainly Kurdish southeast to check reports that Muslim fundamentalists are spreading propaganda in schools."[181]

This disturbing information comes during a time when between 400-500 people have been killed in the other aspect of this movement, which has come to be collectively known as "Hezbollah."[182] These killings actually began in 1987, but appear to be gaining momentum more recently.

The name "Hezbollah," or "Party of God," is notorious among Western experts and lay persons as the Iranian backed terrorist group responsible for several horrific terrorist acts. Most notable among these are the suicide bombing of

---

[178]"State Seen To Act Against Islamists in Politics," Turkish Probe, FBIS, 9 Mar 93.

[179]Ibid.

[180]FBIS, 31 Aug 92.

[181]"Hizbullah Sentiment Seen Spreading: Unsolved Murders Rise," Turkish Daily News, FBIS, 9 Mar 93.

[182]Other spellings include "Hizbullah" and "Hezbullah." Ibid.

the U.S. Marine Barracks in Lebanon in October 1983 and the kidnappings of notable Western figures in Lebanon, such as Terry Anderson.

Turkish journalist Ismet G. Imset, who is recognized in Turkey for his insight on terrorist matters and access to important terrorist leaders, has described the nature of these murders. First, the targets for this violence are essentially all ethnic Kurds. Second, they are all considered by the radical right to be combatants in the state's war against the separatist PKK by virtue of either their political activism, or by actually taking up arms in the fight. The victims of this violence have not only included the common man in southeast Turkey, but also politicians from the pro-Kurdish People's Toil Party (Halkin Emek Partisi or HEP), Erdal Inonu's Social Democratic Populist Party (Sosyal Demokrat Halkici Parti), under which several HEP members ran for parliament in 1991, various local politicians, and journalists.[183] Third, as Imset wrote, "a majority of targets have no protection and are killed while alone either driving their cars or trucks or while crossing the street walking to the neighborhood grocer or

---

[183]Ismet G. Imset, "Terrorist Acts in Southeast Detailed," Turkish Daily News, FBIS, 27 May 92.

sitting in their office."[184] Almost all of the victims where killed by a shot in the back of the head with a single bullet, or by being "sprayed with bullets in the street."[185] Torture is often an ingredient in this violence. Finally, to the distress of the government, human rights organizations, and the international press, these murders have gone unsolved. This has raised the specter of state involvement or acquiescence.

The circumstantial evidence supporting suspicions of complicity in these murders by security forces associated with the state is worrisome. Some local pro-Kurdish officials in the region claim that while 4,000 "separatist suspects" (ostensibly PKK supporters) were arrested in a six month period between January and June 1992, not one suspect of this recent right-wing violence has been detained.[186] In the town of Silvan, a center for this violence which has already claimed 20 victims, not a single culprit has been caught according to one HEP official.[187] Additionally, it was said by this same HEP official that, "security forces first searched the people of the town and disarmed everyone. After

---

[184]Points 1,2 and 3 are from Imset, IBID.

[185]Ibid.

[186]Ibid.

[187]Ibid.

this, the Hezbollah started its activities."[188] This suspicion of state involvement, indifference, or an inability to curb the violence against suspected Pro-PKK supporters, led the locals Kurds to create the name "Hizbul-Contra." "Contra" in this instance, implies counter-guerrillas supported by the state.

One terrorist group referred to by the press as Hezbollah insists its name is the Islamic Liberation Movement (Islamic Kurtulus Hareketi or IKH).[189] According to one member interviewed, Hezbollah is a name which this organization is not yet worthy of using, but which they aspire to eventually use as, "Iran is an example and guide" to this group.[190] However, group members emphatically claim they do not receive instructions from Iran. As one IKH terrorist said, "We do not need instructions from any country. The Koran is our program and rule."[191]

Based on what one Turkish newspaper cites as official records, this organization was established in 1987 in the

---

[188]Ibid.

[189]"'Hizbullah Militant' Interviewed on Struggle," Cumhuriyet, FBIS, 16 Feb 93.

[190]Ibid.

[191]Ibid.

town of Batman.[192] Batman lies approximately 60 miles East of the important town of Diyarbakir, where the Super-Governor and his headquarters control the state's efforts against Kurdish separatism in the Extraordinary Situation Area. Since 1987 though, Hezbollah activities have spread to numerous cities throughout the southeast primarily, and in other regions of the country. Areas of Hezbollah activity are now said to include the following: Van, Mardin, Silvan, Nusaybin, Midyat, Idil, Ceylanpinar, Kiziltepe, Erzerum, Sakarya, Kayseri, Konya, Adana, Kahramanmaras, Istanbul and Ankara.[193]

The objective of this secretive group is said to be the, establishment of an "Islamic Kurdish State in Turkey."[194] It follows from this goal that the IKH will consequently be pitted against both the PKK and the state.

For the IKH, the PKK is seen as "Islam's enemy," and guilty of attempting to, "create an atheist community, supporting the communist system, trying to divide the people through chauvinist activities, and directing pressure on the

---

[192]FBIS, 16 Feb 93.

[193]"PKK-Hizbullah 'Political Feud' Viewed", Hurriyet, FBIS, 10 Feb 93.

[194]FBIS, 16 Feb 93.

Muslim People."[195] On the other hand, Abdullah Ocalan, the leader of the PKK, has said previously that he would not tolerate the existence of other organizations attempting to establish a Kurdish State in Turkey for fear of weakening his movement and its efforts.

As for fighting the state, one Hizbullah militant remarked:

> We have one and only one objective: We will destroy superstition and fulfill the commands of the Koran. God's laws are a constitution for millions and millions of believers in Islam...Our objective is to establish a state for the Muslims."[196]

As the Turkish Republic is officially secular, confrontation resulting from these conflicting goals must also ensue.

Simultaneous to this violence, "pro-Hezbollah" cassette tapes are being distributed throughout Turkey by a business located in the southeastern town of Malatya.[197] Some of the messages on these cassettes include the following:

"We are the Hizbullah-the party of God."

"The Jihad, or a Holy (Islamic) war, is an obligation irrespective of age."

"We will impose our Shari'ah."

---

[195]FBIS, 10 Feb 93.

[196]Ibid.

[197]Ibid.

95

"Hail to the believers of the Hizbullah. Hail to those rising up against blasphemy. Hail to those who tear down icons. Hail to those fighting for the case of Islam. Hail to the glorious, supreme Hizbullah."[198]

On the surface at least, the Hezbollah movement, with its goal of establishing a Muslim state is a threat to both the PKK and the state. Growing popular support also seems to be on the side of this emerging terrorist group. With 400-500 murders ascribed to this Hezbollah movement, and with the list of victims growing daily, how should this information be interpreted in the context of determining the strength of Islamic fundamentalism in Turkey?

B. UNDERSTANDING THE NEW VIOLENCE

It would appear from the proceeding examples that Islamic fundamentalism is an increasingly dangerous problem in a region already plagued with political violence. However, to place the true extent of this problem in perspective, it is necessary to understand what the "Hezbollah" movement actually represents.

"Hezbollah," "Hezbul-contra," or "counterguerrilla" is being used by the Turkish press and the local residents as both a reference to a specific group, such as the IKH, and as a generic term to describe all of this violence.

---

[198]Ibid.

Significantly, in the generic sense, the Hezbollah movement is actually a reference to a conglomeration of several counter-PKK, terrorist groups. While one of these terrorist groups in this Hezbollah movement, the IKH, actually espouses radical Islamic messages, another is merely Islamic oriented and can not be labeled as Islamic fundamentalist. Still another is staunchly supportive of the state, and a fourth, the Grey Wolves or "Idealists," are ultra-nationalists[199]. As all of these groups suspected of involvement in the anti-Kurdish/PKK killings are collectively described by the press as "Hezbollah," and as Hezbollah is associated in Western minds as the notorious Iranian backed organization comprised of true Islamic fundamentalists, confusion in Western circles is bound to ensue.

The result of this confusion is that the power and extent of Islamic fundamentalist sentiments in southeast Turkey will almost assuredly be exaggerated. Violence which is truly anti-PKK, and in some instances vehemently defensive of Ataturk's principles, is wrapped up in a name laden with Islamic fundamentalist symbolism. This confusion is exacerbated by similarities among all of these groups

---

[199]"'Radical Right' Preparing For Clashes With PKK," Paris AFP, FBIS, 9 Jul 92, and "Youth Organization Prepares To Clash With PKK," SABAH, FBIS, 9 Jul 92.

placed under the rubric of Hezbollah in their overlapping areas of operation, methods, motives, and victim selection. This makes it very difficult to separate the violence and other actions of the radical Islamic IKH, from non-fundamentalist entities which are fighting for the state. Nevertheless, if these events are to be accurately interpreted, instead of attributing these 400-500 murders solely to "Hezbollah," ostensibly Islamic fundamentalist actions when placed under this rubric, blame for this violence must also be placed on terrorist groups vehemently supportive of the state,

C. THE ANATOLIA PEOPLE'S FRONT

One organization fighting the PKK, which is described as "counterguerrillas," is the Anatolia People's Front (Anadolu Halk Cehphesi or AHC).[200] This group is said to consist of approximately 500 armed members. It has admitted to killings in Batman, the town in which the fundamentalist IKH was founded, Silvan, Nusaybin, Diyarbakir and Bingol, but refuses to comment on the exact number of people it has killed.[201] As with the Islamic fundamentalist IKH, the AHC also is waging a war against the PKK. An anonymous AHC

---

[200]"'Anatolia People's Front' Said to Be Force Fighting PKK," Tercuman, FBIS, 8 Mar 93.

[201]Part Five: AHC Leader Interview," Tercuman, FBIS, 12 Mar 93.

leader had the following to say about this organization's
goals:

> We are people that have come forth from the bosom of
> the people of Anatolia to take revenge, to ask for the
> account of certain things by the PKK. I am the people, the
> people is me. I cannot kill myself. The guerrillas are
> killing people regardless of whether or not they
> brandish a gun. **We are only killing those who have
> taken up arms against the state and who are working to
> destroy the state.** Among our targets are those who openly
> support the PKK. For us, they are PKK militants. Being
> constrained by the fetters of democracy, the state is
> unable to do anything against the individuals who attempt
> to undermine the state and impair the existing order.
> Therefore, we took this duty upon ourselves, and are doing
> what is necessary[202]

Apart from its similarities with the Islamic
fundamentalist IKH in operating areas and in opposing the
Marxist-Leninist PKK, the AHC is clearly pro-state. This is
absolutely different from the IKH's platform. As the
interviewer of the AHC leader remarked, "These people deeply
revere the state. Their eyes glistened when they spoke about
'Kemalism' [the ideology of Kemal Ataturk]."[203] Naturally
then, lumping the actions of the AHC under any sort of
"Hezbollah" or similar category associated with Islamic
fundamentalism, is to incorrectly ascribe strength to the
radical Islamicist movement in the southeast, which is
actually supportive of the state.

---

[202]"Part Four: AHC Leader Interview," Tercuman, FBIS, 11 Mar
93. Empasis added.

[203]FBIS, 8 Mar 93.

As for the AHC's relationship with the IKH, the AHC leader had the following to say in response:

> It is a completely different entity. They are a religious society that arms itself against the irreligious PKK and have gotten fed up with the PKK. They are people who have armed themselves in desparation from the state's helplessness and have begun a war against the PKK. These are believing Muslims. They have no cooperation or ties with us.[204]

This quote, when coupled with the above views of the AHC, might be interpreted to mean the wave of anti-PKK violence could be divided into two approaches. One approach would be the Islamic fundamentalist view of the IKH, which opposes the PKK because of its "irreligiousness." The second approach would be the AHC's view of attacking the PKK because it threatens the Kemalist vision of Turkey. However, this assessment would also be incorrect. The AHC is also comprised of religious elements separate from Hizbullah. The following is a quote by the AHC leader on this matter:

> What the PKK calls the Hizbulcontra [from Hizbullah and Counterguerrilla] formation is in fact the Islami Yumruk [The Islamic Fist], which is a component of the Muslim fighters. The Islamic Yumruk is an organization attached to AHC. The only difference is that they like the Hizbullah and appreciate Hizbullah's religious devotion, but work independently of Hizbullah. They work with us.[205]

This statement makes it obvious that the argument can not be made that this "Hezbollah" violence is a black and

---

204 FBIS, 12 Mar 93.

205 Ibid.

100

white issue divisible between two elements, one supportive of radical Islamic values, the other staunchly Kemalist. As the existence of the Islamic Fist demonstrates, terrorism based on Islamic values need not necessarily be opposed to the secular state.

Since the Islamic Fist is primarily combatting the PKK due to religious differences, while at the same time is a component of the staunchly Kemalist AHC, it logically follows that this sub-group of the AHC is not interested in destroying the secular state. If it were, it could have joined forces with the IKH or acted on its own. Hence, although the Islamic Fist is obviously religious, it is can not be described as a fundamentalist threat. What begins to emerge from this picture then is a movement which is secular, and in some instances religious. However, the religious sentiment in this issue, as the Islamic Fist demonstrates, is not equivalent to fundamentalism. This raises the question of just how important the Islamic fundamentalist component of the movement is in the totality of this violence. Is the name Hezbollah, with its symbolism of Iranian backed terrorism, really a misnomer ascribed to a smaller Islamic fundamentalist element within a larger secular and religious (not fundamentalist) reaction to the PKK?

It would be difficult to provide a precise answer to these questions without knowing the true strengths of the individual terrorist groups involved. However, there are indications among the gaps in the available information which suggests the Islamic fundamentalist terrorist element in the Hezbollah movement is, in fact, the least important aspect of this anti-PKK reaction.

First, it should not be overlooked that there is no significant fundamentalist movement in the region which exists outside of the PKK issue. When examining this matter and questioning the importance of Islamic fundamentalism, it must not be forgotten that the central issue is really one of reaction to PKK violence. This is the common thread which binds all of this violence together. In other words, if there were a strong undercurrent of Islamic fundamentalism in the region, why has there been a conspicuous absence of any terrorist organization reflective of this sentiment, which is able to survive solely on the appeal of Islamic fundamentalism, and without resorting to focusing on the PKK as the heart of their existence?

Second, as already noted, the rhetoric of the Islamic fundamentalist IKH is critical of both the PKK and the state. From interviews with IKH members, it is known this group has as its broader goal the establishment of a Muslim

state.[206] Yet, if the IKH philosophy of establishing a
Muslim state is the most important element of the Hezbollah
movement, why, as the PKK is quick to point out, are the
actions of this movement totally concentrated against
separatist activities and not also the state?[207]

Certainly, from the available information there is
indisputably an Islamic fundamentalist component to this
movement. Consequently, the answer to this question can not
be based on dismissing Islamic fundamentalist sentiment as
non-existent. More logically, Islamic fundamentalist
sentiment in this Hezbollah movement is the weaker element,
and as mentioned, is probably unable to sustain itself to
any appreciable degree without its focus remaining fixed
against the PKK.

It is also probably too weak as an organization to
attack both the PKK and the state, and may consequently be
attempting to secure its position first, before attempting
any actions against the state. If this Islamic
fundamentalist element were sufficiently strong enough to
challenge both the state and the PKK, would it stand to
reason that it would strengthen the hand of the state it
hopes to overthrow by concentrating on that state's most

---

[206]FBIS, 16 Feb 93.

[207]FBIS, 10 Feb 93.

pressing problem to internal security? If the Islamic fundamentalist terrorists of the Hezbollah movement were actually the strongest group ivolved in this violence, this would place their membership at figures greater than the AHC's 500 armed men. Any such figure above 500 armed men would surely be able to expend some its resources in attacks against the state, even if only symbolic ones. Yet, the victims in this new wave of violence remain ethnic Kurds associated with the PKK.

The issue of tactics also raise questions about who is doing most of the killing. The AHC is extremely candid about their methods:

> We abduct a person at a convienent moment, once we are certain he is cooperating with the PKK. We take him to a desolate place, we explain to him that he has betrayed the state, and we read out his crimes. After reminding him that the penalty for this is death, we fire a single bullet into his head...We ambush those we cannot abduct and after having dispatched him with a single bullet, we scatter to our cell-houses in the city.[208]

These methods, with the exception of killing someone in an ambush with "a single bullet," which sounds like an exageration, are consistent with the reported manner in which most of the victims of this violence are said to have been killed.

---

[208]FBIS, 12 Mar 93.

On the other hand, the IKH claims to have been involved in the infamous murder of Bahriye Ucok in Ankara in 1990.[209] Ucok was a prominent female parliamentarian, known for her pro-secularist and feminist work. Attacking someone like Ucok would be consistent with the IKH's professed philosophy. However, the sophisticated bomb which killed Ucok is said to have been the responsibility of the transnational terrorist group, the Islamic Jihad. This was determined by security officials who discovered similarities between the sophisticated Ucok bombing and previous Islamic Jihad bomb attacks on several diplomats and an American service member, all of which occurred in Ankara.[210]

This discrepancy as to who is actually responsible for the Ucok bombing raises two possibilities. First, the Islamic Jihad and the IKH are one in the same organization. However, if this were the case, it would be logical to expect that at least some of the victims murdered in Hezbollah violence in the southeast would be killed through sophisticated bombings similar to the one which killed Ucok. This technique might not be efficient or even plausible for the murder of a villager or lesser target, but certainly, larger cities like Diyarbakir where there are politicians

---

[209]FBIS, 16 Feb 93.

[210]FBIS, 30 Oct 91.

and journalists, would present ample opportunity to place this deadly method into practice. This is simply not happening according to Imset. The second and more plausible explanation is that the IKH took responsibility for a murder they did not commit.

On one hand then, there are the actions of the AHC, whose professed methods are consistent with the reported methods of death for most of the victims of Hezbollah actions in the southeast. On the other hand, there is the IKH, which has claimed responsibility for a murder they almost certainly did not commit, a sophistication yet to be shown in the violence in the southeast, and a method not employed in these murders.

As for the religious grass-roots movement mentioned earlier, it appears that the issue of the PKK is also involved in this matter. There are definitely Islamic fanatics in the region, but according to the Deputy Director of Religious Affairs, in this matter the PKK is singled out as the guilty party exploiting religious feelings.[211] As the director said, "PKK militants were exploiting the religious feelings of the people by pretending that they were prepared to 'die for their kinsfolk.'"[212] In some cases, "PKK

---

[211]FBIS, 31 Aug 92.

[212]Ibid.

separatists have even spread the idea that the prophet Abraham was of Kurdish origin."[213] What appears as the beginnings of a grass-roots Islamic fundamentalist movement then, is also simply another component of the struggle between the state and PKK. In this instance, the PKK is attempting to misdirect the piety of the population by discrediting the state's appointed religious leaders. How serious is this problem? The Turkish Interior Minister Ismet Sezgin did not appear very concerned. His feelings about this matter are clear from the following quote:

> They [Islamic fundamentalists] are terror organizations, and they have the same objectives: They want to destroy the state and overthrow the government. We are taking action against this terror with all our might. However, **this antisecular movement is not a movement that must be taken seriously.**"[214]

Furthermore, the Deputy Director's recommendation for dealing with this problem was to broadcast more religious programs on the local televisions, "because the holy Koran is based on love, brotherhood, tolerance and justice." These words and actions do not seem like those of someone who is facing a serious Islamic fundamentalist threat.

---

[213]Ibid.

[214]Emphasis added. "Interior Minister Views Kurds, PKK, Fundamentalism," Vienna DER STANDARD, FBIS, 13-14 Mar 93.

D. CONCLUDING THOUGHTS ON THE HEZBOLLAH MOVEMENT

In time, as more information becomes available concerning the Hezbollah movement, the true nature of this violence will be exposed. In the meantime, confusion arising from the inappropriate use of the name "Hezbollah" with this violence is sure to arouse further concerns in the West that Turkey is facing a serious Islamic fundamentalist threat. It may be that as further details are acquired about the strength of these terrorist organizations, the radical Islamic, IKH terrorist group is proven to be the dominant element of this movement, and a true threat to the state. Until a conclusive answer is discovered, as pointed out previously, there are several reasons to judge with caution the warnings of those who would prematurely say that Hezbollah violence is an Islamic fundamentalist threat to the state. The questionable veracity of the IKH is just one of these reasons.

Finally, the common thread behind this new violence must be kept clearly in mind. It is the PKK which is the present threat to the state and the focus of all of this violence. In spite of the publicity the Hezbollah movement may eventually receive, it is the Marxist-Leninist PKK which has killed over 5,000 people, and challenges the state for control of its southeastern provinces. Compared to this violence, the Hezbollah movement, whether it is proven to be predominantly state-supportive, Islamic fundamentalist, or a combination of both, is merely a side show at the moment. Consequently, while it may be fashionable to find evidence of the green threat to Turkey, the evidence supports the fact that the leftists are presently the most dangerous challenge to the state.

IV. CONCLUDING REMARKS ON THE ACCURACY OF ISLAMIC FUNDAMENTALISM IN TURKEY

As mentioned earlier, in Turkey, a country of 55.4 million people, 99 percent of whom are Muslim, it would be ludicrous to suggest there is no support for Islamic activism. That has never been the message of this paper. There are true signs of politically active, often radical, Muslim elements in Turkey. For the West, the most visible of these fringe elements of Islamic activism are the radical Islamic terrorist groups. They are likely to continue with their deadly terrorist attacks which will present a risk to certain individuals. Prominent journalists, government officials, others who champion the cause of secularism, and foreign military and diplomatic personnel appear to be their present targets. These attacks should not be taken lightly. Significantly though, these terrorist actions represent a real threat to only small groups of select people. This is altogether different from threatening the stability of the state.

I have also not attempted to paint the picture that Turkey is completely secular, either in its government, or society in general. There has been a synthesis of the moderate right and even the left with Islamic political parties. This has occurred because, as historian Martin Kramer noted, these parties, "began to appreciate the political benefits that accrued from inclusion of Islamic planks in their platforms." These benefits derived from the use of Islam and its symbols would not exist if Islam in Turkey were dead.

Even the popular Turkish media, targets for some radical Islamic terrorist groups, have not divorced themselves entirely from Islam. When the newspaper Sabah decided last June that it would publish during the Kurban Bayrami (Feast of Sacrifice) holiday, which is against Turkish law, it raised a storm of controversy among the associations of journalists in the country. The leader of the Istanbul Journalists' Association went so far as to criticize Sabah for going against, "all moral principles." It may be that the "principles" implied to refer to breaking the law, but it is interesting none the less that Turkey's other major newspapers did not follow Sabah's example and that such a law would even exist.

The message I am attempting to communicate is that the threat of radical Islam in Turkey appears drastically out of proportion to the evidence presented in the media and by some Western scholars. Neither the success of Islamic politicians under Ozal, the symbolic actions they were able to achieve, the Prosperity Party's showing in November 1991, the emerging Hezbollah movement, nor other factors considered in this paper, when examined more thoroughly, suggest a serious threat to Turkey's stability.

The threat from Islamic activism in Turkey today is even less realistic than implied in the popular Western media when the role of the Turkish military as protector's of Ataturk's legacy is brought into focus. The Turkish armed forces have gone to great lengths to ensure its officer and conscript ranks remain a force free from politically active Islamic soldiers, as well as extremists of the left. Measures have included extensive investigations of all ranks and services and mass dismissals from the service of anyone thought to harbor extremist feelings. With such stringent measures, the Turkish military will remain a force free to counter-balance any extremist attempt to upset the secular cornerstone laid by Ataturk. The Turkish military's interventions into civilian rule in 1960, 1971, and 1980, stand as testaments that only limited interference with Ataturk's secular legacy will be tolerated.

The criticism leveled at the Western media and some Western scholars is not to suggest these people are disingenuous with the information they present. Rather, the inaccurate assessment of the threat of radical Islam in

Turkey demonstrates the much larger misunderstanding of the phenomenon of "fundamentalism," and the Islamic World in general. As demonstrated in the examination of the growth of Islamic banks, and the turban in Turkey, the presence of Islam in a politically charged topic is not conclusive proof of Islamic fundamentalism. The symbols and religion of Islam apply to a wide variety of situations, and the solutions derived from the application of Islam are not automatically antithetical to Western values. Islamic symbols, just as those of other religions, are malleable and subject to various interpretations. Some of these interpretations will stand against what is believed correct and modern in the West, others will mirror Western values. This was demonstrated in the use of Islam and the turban to support "Islamic feminism."

Still other groups will promote Islam and co-opt its symbols and power to advance Western visions of modernity. Ozal attempted this by using the Islamic vote in his coalition to overpower his main rivals and enact his Western vision. His acceptance of and assistance to Islamic banking in Turkey is argued to have been with the intent to create a more competitive system which would foster increased democratization. Even the military, the guardian of

Ataturk's secular reforms, promoted Islam as a tool against the real threat of the left.

It must also be recognized that the Islamic fundamentalists are themselves not a monolithic group and that they vary in beliefs and actions. Furthermore, those who support these groups do so for a variety of reasons. Islamic groups do not only preach for a return of the sharia, or protection of the umma. Many involved in this movement, such as Erbakan, appeal to peoples' disgust of their economic desparation, promising a better tomorrow, not unlike every other politician. The piety of some of these Islamic activists, when considered against the corruption prevalent in many Third World Islamic nations must also strike a deep chord among the population.

Western scholars and the media must therefore come to a more comprehensive understanding of this phenomenon if they are to ever understand it. Those who represent Islam as a force to be used against the West do not represent the majority of Muslims anymore than intolerant Christian and Jewish fringe groups in this country represent the U.S. population. Those who support the fundamentalists do so for a variety of reasons. Those who use Islam as a tool are not necessarily Islamic fundamentalists or even devout Muslims. And most importantly, Islam is not equivalent to Islamic fanaticism. Only when these and other lessons about Islamic culture are inculcated in Western attitudes can we improve the accuracy of our understanding of this phenomenon we have come to know as "Islamic fundamentalism."

www.ingramcontent.com/pod-product-compliance
Lightning Source LLC
Chambersburg PA
CBHW080304290526
45790CB00005B/1926